Test Prep Reading Book for CASAS Reading STEPS Level E—Forms 629R and 630R

Turning Learners into Proficient Readers while Preparing them for CASAS Reading STEPS Level E—Forms 629R & 630R

By

COACHING FOR BETTER LEARNING

TABLE OF CONTENTS

PREFACE

Dear Instructors,

Get ready to transform your ESL classroom with our *Test Prep Reading Book for CASAS Reading STEPS Level E,* specifically designed for the Form 629R & 630R reading comprehension tests. This essential tool aligns with the English Language Proficiency Standards (ELPS) for Adult Education. It satisfies the National Reporting System (NRS) and Workforce Innovation and Opportunity Act (WIOA) expectations, ensuring your ESL students are on the path to success.

This reading textbook is more than just a teaching aid; it is a comprehensive program tailored to bolster reading comprehension among ESL learners. With a structured layout of five units and one practice test, totaling 15 learner-centered reading lessons, your students will navigate essential topics like basic communication, consumer economics, community resources, health, employment, government, and law.

Leverage Bloom's Taxonomy's six levels of objectives and competencies (remembering, understanding, applying, analyzing, evaluating, and creating) to enhance your teaching methods. Each lesson in the book is a stepping stone that equips you with the strategies to teach reading effectively, focusing on important skills such as identifying main ideas, uncovering details, making inferences, summarizing content, applying knowledge, understanding the author's perspective, and contextual vocabulary. The clarity and depth of the lessons will enable you to deliver content that resonates with your students and solidifies their understanding.

Finally, this textbook isn't just about reading—it's about providing your students with the academic and life skills they need to thrive. As they progress through the book, they'll gain valuable insights and abilities to navigate the complexities of community life, family responsibilities, and the workplace. By using this book, you'll be equipping your students for standardized testing and real-world challenges.

INTRODUCTION

Dear Students,

This book is your guide to preparing for the CASAS Reading STEPS level E test. It's filled with lessons to help you read better.

The book has five units and one practice test. Each unit has two to four lessons, for a total of 15 lessons. The lessons teach important skills like basic communication, understanding money, finding community help, staying healthy, finding a job, and learning about government and laws. These skills will help you in many parts of your life.

When you read this book, you will interact with different texts and information about reading and real-world activities. After you read, you will answer questions. These questions make sure you understand the main points, details, the writer's thoughts, and the words they use.

Remember, reading is a skill that gets better as you use it. This book is a unique tool. It will teach you about school and life and give you information to help you in your community, with your family, and at work.

Good luck as you practice your reading! Every lesson you finish will take you closer to your goals.

Reading Strategies:

Here are ten ways you can improve your reading comprehension skills:

1. Preview the text: Look at titles and subtitles to get an idea of what you will read.

2. Set a purpose: Decide why you are reading. Is it to answer a question or learn something new?

3. Read aloud daily: This can help you better understand texts. The more you read, the better you will get.

4. Use pictures: They can help you guess and understand the text.

5. Re-read: If you don't understand something, read it again.

6. Summarize: After reading, tell yourself what the text was about.

7. Ask questions: While reading, ask, "Who, what, where, when, why, and how?"

8. Make connections: Relate the text to your own life or things you already know.

9. Learn to infer: Guess what the author means based on clues in the text.

10. Use a dictionary: If you don't know a word, look it up.

Vocabulary Building:

Here are seven strategies to increase your vocabulary:

Strategy	Description
Find synonyms.	Look for words that mean the same as new words you find.
Use the words.	Try to use new words in sentences of your own.
Make flashcards.	Write new words on cards with their meanings.
Create a vocabulary journal.	Keep a notebook of new words and their meanings.
Read regularly.	The more you read, the more words you will learn.
Learn word parts.	Study prefixes, suffixes, and roots to understand more words.
Play word games.	Games like crosswords can help you learn new words.

Keep going; you can do it!

Lesson 1: Consumer Protection

Objectives:

1. Students will read and answer questions about various aspects of consumer protection.
2. Students will use new words to complete exercises about consumer protection measures.

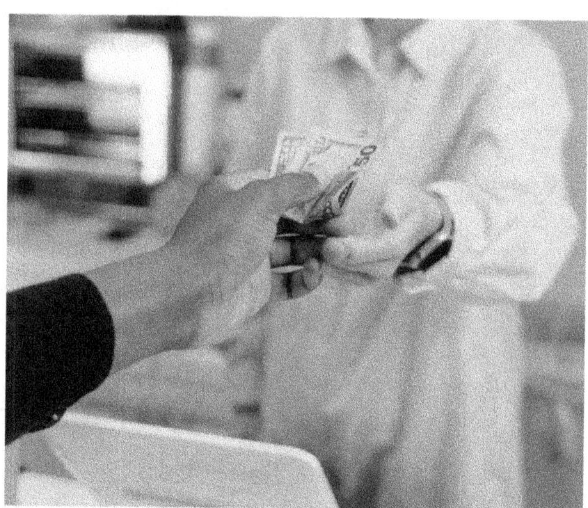

Exercise 1- Draw a line connecting each word to its correct definition.

Word	Meaning
1. Advocate	a. Someone who supports a cause or person
2. Fraud	b. Money returned to a customer after dissatisfaction
3. Warranty	c. A legal agreement between parties
4. Contract	d. Deception intended to gain money
5. Scam	e. A formal expression of dissatisfaction
6. Consumer	f. A dishonest scheme for profit
7. Complaint	g. A guarantee or promise about a product's quality
8. Refund	h. A person who buys goods/services

Better Business Bureau

The Better Business Bureau (BBB) is a nonprofit organization that aims to build trust between consumers and businesses. Founded over 100 years ago, the BBB is recognized for its role in monitoring company behavior, verifying business legitimacy, and assisting consumers in making smart decisions. By reporting scams and rating businesses, the BBB strives to help consumers avoid fraud and dishonest practices.

The BBB also offers a platform where consumers can file complaints against businesses. This process is simple and effective, encouraging companies to respond to consumer issues. The ratings given by the BBB to businesses are based on various factors, such as how businesses handle complaints and how honest they are. Therefore, using BBB ratings can be helpful for consumers when deciding which businesses to trust.

Comprehension Questions:

1. What is the main purpose of the BBB?

2. When was the BBB started?

3. How does the BBB help consumers avoid fraud?

4. How can the BBB ratings be useful for consumers?

5. Why is the BBB important?

6. How does the author feel about the BBB?

Consumer Protection Rights

Consumer protection rights are rules that make sure people are treated fairly and have access to safe products. For example, consumers have the right to know what is in the food they purchase, to receive correct information about services, and to be protected from false advertising. The Federal Trade Commission (FTC) is responsible for enforcing these rights.

In addition to the FTC, state agencies also have their own consumer protection offices. These agencies help to handle local issues that may involve scams, misleading advertisements, or unsafe products. Understanding these consumer rights is crucial for anyone making purchases, as it shows what to expect from businesses and what actions to take if those expectations are not met.

Comprehension Questions:

1. What are consumer protection rights?

____

2. What is the role of the FTC?

____

3. What is the author's purpose in describing consumer rights?

____

4. How do state consumer protection agencies support the FTC?

____

5. Why are consumer protection rights important?

____

6. What is the author's view on consumer protection?

____

Exercise 4- Read the tips below before answering the questions.

7 Tips on Consumer Protection

1. Keep receipts for all major purchases.

2. Be cautious of unsolicited phone calls or emails.

3. Research businesses before making a purchase.

4. Report fraud to the Federal Trade Commission.

5. Read all contracts carefully before signing.

6. Understand your right to cancel certain purchases.

7. Never give out personal information to unknown parties.

Comprehension Questions:

1. What is the main purpose of these tips?

____

2. Which tip would help you most in avoiding online scams?

____

3. Why is keeping receipts important?

____

4. How are "reading contracts carefully" and "researching businesses" similar?

____

5. What is the author's purpose in providing these tips?

____

6. What does the author believe about giving personal information to people you don't know?

____

Exercise 5- Fill in the blanks with the correct words: *complaint, fraud, refund, contract, scam* and *consumer.*

1. The email was a _______________________________ asking for my bank details.

2. I had to file a _______________________________ because the product was faulty.

3. The FTC works to prevent _______________________________ and protect consumers.

4. It's important to read a _______________________________ carefully before you sign it.

5. The company offered a full _______________________________ after my complaint.

6. A _______________________________ is someone who buys goods or services.

Exercise 6- Writing

Write a paragraph to summarize what you know and learned about consumer protection in your own words.

____

____

ANSWER KEYS

Exercise 1- Vocabulary Matching:

1. Advocate – a. Someone who supports a cause or person
2. Fraud – d. Deception intended to gain money
3. Warranty – g. A guarantee or promise about a product's quality
4. Contract – c. A legal agreement between parties
5. Scam – f. A dishonest scheme for profit
6. Consumer – h. A person who buys goods/services
7. Complaint – e. A formal expression of dissatisfaction
8. Refund – b. Money returned to a customer after dissatisfaction

Exercise 2- Text 1:

1. The main purpose is to build trust between consumers and businesses.
2. It was started over 100 years ago.
3. It reports scams and rates businesses.
4. They help consumers decide which businesses to trust.
5. It helps people avoid fraud, ensures businesses are honest, and encourages businesses to respond to consumer complaints.
6. The author believes the BBB is effective in helping consumers.

Exercise 3- Text 2:

1. These are rules that make sure consumers are treated fairly and have access to safe products.
2. The FTC ensures that people follow consumer protection rights.
3. The author's purpose is to educate consumers on their rights and the agencies that protect them.
4. State consumer protection agencies handle local issues like scams, false advertisements and unsafe products.
5. They are essential for helping people know what to expect from businesses and give them a way to act if businesses do not meet these expectations.
6. The author sees consumer protection as essential because it helps people make fair and safe choices when buying products and services.

Exercise 4- Consumer Protection Tips

1. To help consumers protect themselves from scams.
2. "Be cautious of unsolicited phone calls or emails" would help most.
3. Receipts are important for proving purchases or if you need to return or exchange something.
4. Both actions involve gathering and understanding important information before making a decision.
5. To guide consumers on how to protect themselves from scams and stay safe when buying products or services.
6. It should be avoided to prevent fraud.

Exercise 5- Fill-in-the-Blanks:

1. scam
2. complaint
3. fraud
4. contract
5. refund
6. consumer

Lesson 2: Maintaining Personal Possessions

Objectives

1. Students will read and answer questions related to the maintenance and use of personal possessions, such as cars, houses, and computers.
2. Students will use new words to complete exercises about the maintenance of personal possessions.

Exercise 1- Draw a line connecting each word to its correct definition.

Word	Meaning
1. Maintenance	a. An item that someone owns
2. Inspection	b. Actions taken to stop problems before they happen
3. Routine	c. A device or machine usually for the home
4. Property	d. The process of keeping something in good condition
5. Repair	e. A direction on how to do something
6. Preventive	f. A careful examination to make sure everything is working correctly
7. Instruction	g. To fix something that is damaged
8. Appliance	h. Regular or usual procedure

Exercise 2- Read the text below before answering the questions.

Car Maintenance Essentials

Owning a car is a big responsibility. To keep it in good condition, it is important to perform routine maintenance. This includes checking the oil, replacing filters, and making sure the tires have enough air. Taking these steps regularly helps to prevent major issues and keeps the car running smoothly. Preventive care is always better than facing expensive repairs later.

Another key to car maintenance is following the manufacturer's instructions. The owner's manual provides a schedule for oil changes and other essential tasks. Staying on top of these responsibilities can extend the life of your car. Additionally, if the car is under warranty, following these maintenance routines is required to keep the warranty valid.

Comprehension Questions:

1. What is the main topic of the text?

____

2. Why is preventive care important?

____

3. What is the author's purpose in writing this text?

____

4. What might happen if you do not follow the manufacturer's instructions?

____

5. What does the author think about routine maintenance?

____

6. What can be compared to routine maintenance in this text?

____

Exercise 3- Read the text below before answering the questions.

Taking Care of Your Home

A home is one of the biggest investments a person can make. Regular maintenance is key to keeping the home in good condition. This includes simple actions like cleaning gutters, checking the roof for leaks, and testing smoke alarms. Keeping up with these small tasks can prevent big problems down the road. Preventive measures save both time and money in the long term.

Home maintenance also involves understanding when to call a professional. For example, an electrician should fix electrical problems. By recognizing when you need professional help, you ensure your home remains safe and well-maintained. Taking care of your home isn't just about keeping it looking good; it's about ensuring the safety of everyone inside.

Comprehension Questions:

1. What is the main idea of the text?

____

2. What are two preventive measures that help maintain your home?

____

3. Why is preventive maintenance important for a home?

____

4. What is the author's purpose in discussing professional help?

____

5. What inference can be made about ignoring small maintenance tasks?

____

6. How does the author feel about professional help?

____

Exercise 4- Read the text below before answering the questions.

Maintaining Your Computer

Computers are essential tools in today's world, both for work and leisure. To keep a computer functioning well, it is important to do routine maintenance. This includes updating the system, cleaning the hardware, and using antivirus software. These actions help keep your computer secure and operating at its best.

Another aspect of computer maintenance is saving your files. Regularly backing up important files ensures that you do not lose valuable information if the computer stops working. Keeping your computer safe involves not only caring for its hardware but also ensuring your data is secure. By following these basic practices, you can prolong the life of your computer.

Comprehension Questions

1. What is the main focus of this text?

____

2. What is the purpose of updating the system?

____

3. What happens if you do not back up your data?

____

4. How does the author feel about antivirus software?

____

5. What is the author's purpose in writing this text?

____

6. What other maintenance actions are similar to using antivirus software?

____

Exercise 5- Read the tips below before answering the questions.

---

9 Tips on House Maintenance

1. Clean your gutters twice a year.

2. Check your roof for leaks after heavy rain.

3. Test smoke alarms every month.

4. Service your heating system yearly.

5. Keep your lawn trimmed and maintained.

6. Replace worn weatherstripping on windows and doors.

7. Inspect your foundation for cracks regularly.

8. Ensure that pipes are not leaking.

9. Check for pest infestations and take action if needed.

Comprehension Questions

1. What is the main idea of the tips provided?

____

2. What is the author's purpose in providing these tips?

____

3. What can happen if you do not inspect pipes for leaks?

____

4. Which tip would be most useful in preventing water damage?

____

5. How does the author feel about pest control?

____

6. How are servicing your heating system and testing smoke alarms similar?

Exercise 6- Read the tips below before answering the questions.

7 Tips on Car Maintenance
1. Check tire pressure monthly.
2. Change oil as recommended by the manufacturer.
3. Replace air filters regularly.
4. Keep your car clean to prevent rust.
5. Inspect brakes for wear.
6. Check all fluid levels, including coolant.
7. Have regular professional check-ups.

Comprehension Questions

1. What is the main idea of the car maintenance tips?

____

2. What is the purpose of checking tire pressure?

____

3. What could happen if oil is not changed regularly?

____

4. How does the author feel about professional car check-ups?

____

5. What is the author's purpose in providing these car maintenance tips?

____

6. Which tip helps to maintain the car's exterior?

____

Exercise 7- Fill in the blanks with the correct words: repair, maintenance, warranty, preventative, instructions and routine.

1. Regular _________________________________ can help extend the life of your car.

2. It is important to read the _____________________ to understand how to care for an appliance.

3. My car is still under _____________________________, so the repairs were covered.

4. The plumber came to _________________________ the leaking pipe under the sink.

5. The computer needs a _________________________ update to stay secure.

6. It is better to take _________________________ measures than deal with a breakdown.

Exercise 8- Writing

Write a paragraph to summarize what you know and learned about maintaining your possessions.

ANSWER KEYS

Exercise 1- Vocabulary Matching:

1. Maintenance - d. The process of keeping something in good condition
2. Inspection - f. A careful examination to make sure everything is working correctly
3. Routine - h. Regular or usual procedure
4. Property - a. An item that someone owns
5. Repair - g. To fix something that is damaged
6. Preventive - b. Actions taken to stop problems before they happen
7. Instruction - e. A direction on how to do something
8. Appliance - c. A device or machine usually for the home

Exercise 2- Text 1:

1. The main topic of the text is the importance of car maintenance.
2. It helps avoid major issues and costly repairs.
3. The author's purpose is to inform car owners about the importance of routine maintenance and following the manufacturer's instructions.
4. If you do not follow the manufacturer's instructions, it might void the car's warranty and lead to costly repairs.
5. The author believes it is crucial for keeping a car in good condition.
6. In this text, routine maintenance can be compared to preventive care, as both help prevent bigger problems

Exercise 3- Text 2:

1. Regular maintenance is important to keep a home in good condition and prevent big problems.
2. Two preventive measures are cleaning the gutters and testing smoke alarms.
3. It is important for a home because it saves both time and money in the long term.
4. The author's purpose is to explain that certain problems should be fixed by a professional to ensure safety and proper maintenance of the home.
5. They could lead to bigger problems and costly repairs in the future.
6. The author feels that professional help is important and necessary for certain tasks, like electrical issues, to keep the home safe and well-maintained.

Exercise 4- Text 3:

1. The text focuses on how to maintain a computer.
2. Updating the system keeps the computer secure and functioning well.
3. It may lead to the loss of valuable information if the computer stops working.
4. The author thinks it is essential for keeping a computer secure.
5. The author wants to provide information on how to properly maintain a computer.
6. Other maintenance actions similar to using antivirus software include updating the system and cleaning the hardware.

Exercise 5- House Maintenance Tips:

1. The tips are on maintaining a house by performing regular checks and maintenance tasks.
2. The author's purpose is to inform homeowners how to take care of their property effectively.
3. Not doing so can lead to water damage and increased utility bills.
4. Checking your roof for leaks after heavy rain would be most useful.
5. The author thinks it is an important part of home maintenance.
6. They are similar because they can prevent potential fires in the home.

Exercise 6- Car Maintenance Tips:

1. It is to provide information on keeping a car in good condition.
2. Checking tire pressure ensures the car runs efficiently and safely.
3. It could damage the engine and reduce the car's lifespan.
4. The author sees them as necessary for maintaining the health of the car.
5. The author's purpose is to inform car owners on how to care for their vehicles so they run smoothly and last longer.
6. Keeping the car clean to prevent rust is the tip to maintain the car's exterior.

Exercise 7- Fill-in-the-Blanks:

1. maintenance
2. instructions
3. warranty
4. repair
5. routine
6. preventive

REFLECTION ON LEARNING

Answer the following questions and discuss your responses with your teacher or classmates.

1. What reading strategies did you learn or practice in this unit?

2. What new concepts or words did you learn?

3. What reading challenges did you face?

4. What reading strategies do you need to improve?

5. What do you want your teacher to know?

Lesson 1: Using Community Agencies and Services

Objectives

1. Students will read and answer questions about different community agencies and their functions.
2. Students will use new words to complete exercises about community services and their importance in real-life situations.

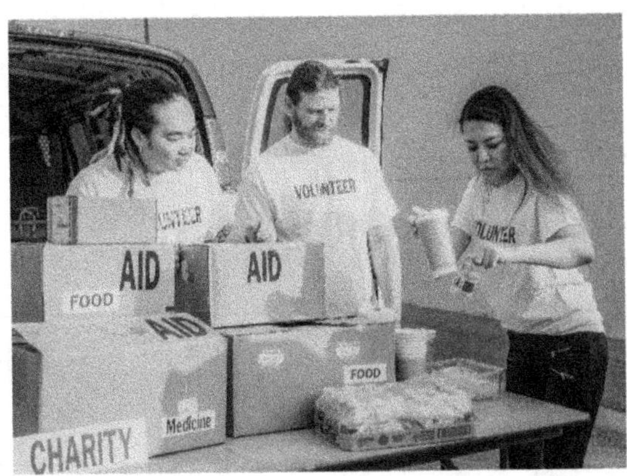

Exercise 1- Draw a line connecting each word to its correct definition.

Word	Meaning
1. Agency	a. Guidance or advice given by a professional
2. Shelter	b. A place helping people in emergency situations
3. Volunteer	c. A place where food is given to those in need
4. Counseling	d. An organization providing a service
5. Food Bank	e. Government support for those in need
6. Hotline	f. Someone who helps without payment
7. Welfare	g. A telephone service for emergencies
8. Crisis Center	h. A place providing temporary housing

The Importance of Community Agencies

Community agencies play a significant role in our society. They provide various services that support people in times of need. For example, shelters offer temporary housing to individuals who are homeless. This helps them have a safe place to stay while they work on improving their situation.

Another important agency is the food bank. Food banks provide essential nutrition to families and individuals who are struggling financially. Without food banks, many people would face hunger on a daily basis. These agencies rely on donations from the community and volunteers who want to make a difference.

Counseling services are also an important part of community agencies. People who are dealing with mental health issues or facing difficult life situations can seek advice from professional counselors. Counseling provides a space for individuals to talk about their problems and receive helpful guidance.

Comprehension Questions:

1. What role do community agencies play in society?

____

2. How do shelters help individuals?

____

3. Why are food banks important for people in need?

____

4. Why might volunteers be crucial for food banks?

____

5. How are food banks and shelters similar?

____

6. What is the author's point of view on counseling services?

____

Exercise 3- Read the text below before answering the questions.

Community Services for Crisis Management

Crisis centers provide immediate help to individuals going through emergencies. These centers have hotlines that anyone can call for urgent support. The staff at crisis centers are trained to provide emotional and practical support to help callers through difficult situations.

Hotlines are not only for emergencies. Some hotlines offer counseling for people dealing with ongoing issues such as addiction or abuse. Because hotlines are anonymous, people feel safer calling without the fear of being judged. This service is vital in giving people the courage to take the first step toward getting help.

Another community service is welfare support. Welfare programs are run by the government to help people who are in financial hardship. These programs may provide food, housing, or healthcare assistance to families and individuals. Welfare is important because it ensures that everyone has basic needs met, especially during tough times.

Comprehension Questions:

1. What kind of help do crisis centers provide?

____

2. Why are hotlines considered important for helping people?

____

3. What can we infer about the role of welfare programs?

____

4. Why might people prefer using hotlines?

____

5. How do hotlines and welfare programs differ in their services?

____

6. What is the author's view on the importance of government welfare?

____

Community Agencies

Agency	Service Provided	Contact Method	Operating Hours	Location
Red Cross	Emergency relief and support	Hotline	24/7	Nationwide
Local Shelter	Temporary housing	In-person registration	9 AM - 5 PM	Downtown
Food Bank	Food distribution	Volunteer program	10 AM - 4 PM	Various locations
Crisis Center	Emotional support and crisis help	Phone hotline	24/7	City Center
Welfare Office	Financial assistance	Appointment	8 AM - 4 PM	City Hall

Comprehension Questions:

1. Which community agency provides emergency relief?

____

2. How can someone access the services of a local shelter?

____

3. Why do you think food banks have volunteer programs?

____

4. Why do you think crisis centers are open 24/7?

____

5. How are the services of the Red Cross and the Welfare Office different?

____

6. Why does the author include both emergency and regular services?

____

Exercise 5- Fill in the blanks with the correct words: crisis center, shelter, food bank, hotline, counseling and welfare.

1. The _________________________ provides temporary housing for those in need.

2. A _________________________ can be used to get immediate help during a crisis.

3. Many people volunteer at the _________________________ to help feed the community.

4. _________________________ services offer professional advice to people in difficult situations.

5. _________________________ programs are important for providing basic needs to those in hardship.

6. The _________________________ has trained staff to support people during emergencies.

Exercise 6- Writing

Write a paragraph to summarize what you know and learned about community agencies and services in your own words.

ANSWER KEYS

Exercise 1- Vocabulary Matching:

- Agency - d. An organization providing a service
- Shelter – h. A place providing temporary housing
- Volunteer – f. Someone who helps without payment
- Counseling – a. Guidance or advice given by a professional
- Food Bank – c. A place where food is given to those in need
- Hotline – g. A telephone service for emergencies
- Welfare – e. Government support for those in need
- Crisis Center - b. A place helping people in emergency situations

Exercise 2- Text 1:

1. They provide various services that support people in times of need.
2. Shelters offer temporary housing to individuals who are homeless.
3. Food banks give essential nutrition to people who are unable to afford food and help them avoid hunger.
4. Volunteers are crucial because they help to collect, organize and distribute food.
5. Both food banks and shelters provide essential support to people in need.
6. The author believes counseling is important for mental well-being because they provide a safe space for individuals to talk about their problems.

Exercise 3- Text 2:

1. Crisis centers provide immediate help to individuals going through emergencies.
2. Hotlines are important because they offer urgent support anonymously.
3. If there were no welfare programs, people in need might struggle to meet basic needs such as food, housing, and healthcare.
4. People may prefer hotlines because they provide a safe, anonymous way to seek help without feeling judged.
5. Hotlines provide immediate emotional support, whereas welfare programs provide practical help, such as food and housing.
6. The author views welfare as a crucial safety net for those in financial hardship.

Exercise 4- Community Agencies:

1. The Red Cross provides emergency relief.
2. They can access the services by registering in person.
3. Food banks have volunteer programs so they can provide the services without the extra cost of paying people to do tasks like organizing and distributing food.
4. Crisis centers are open 24/7 because emergencies can happen at any time.
5. The Red Cross provides emergency relief, while the Welfare Office offers financial assistance.
6. The author does this to show that community agencies help people in urgent situations and also give ongoing support to those who need it.

Exercise 5- Fill-in-the-Blanks:

1. Shelter
2. Hotline
3. Food bank
4. Counseling
5. Welfare
6. Crisis Center

Lesson 2: Leisure Time Activities and Facilities

Objectives:

1. Students will read and answer questions about different leisure time activities and the facilities available in the community.
2. Students will use new words to complete exercises about activities and facilities used during leisure time.

Exercise 1- Draw a line connecting each word to its correct definition.

Word	Meaning
1. Gym	a. The act of joining a club or organization
2. Vacation	b. Someone who trains athletes
3. Facility	c. Free time for relaxation
4. YMCA	d. A period of rest or travel
5. Membership	e. A community center offering activities
6. Sports	f. A place to exercise
7. Coach	g. Physical games or activities
8. Leisure	h. A building or place that provides a service

Exercise 2- Read the text below before answering the questions.

Enjoying Vacation and Leisure Time

Leisure time is essential for maintaining balance in life. People often spend their vacation traveling or relaxing at home. For example, Mary decided to visit her parents in Florida during her vacation. She enjoyed the sunny weather and spent her time reading on the beach.

Sports activities are also a common way to spend leisure time. John loves playing basketball during the weekends. He joined a local basketball league at the YMCA. The coach at the YMCA is experienced, and John appreciates the chance to improve his skills while meeting new friends.

Another popular leisure activity is visiting parks and community centers. These places offer activities like yoga classes, swimming, and picnics. Many people find relaxation and joy in using these facilities, which are often free or require only a small fee. Taking time for leisure activities is not only fun but can help people stay healthy and connected with others.

Comprehension Questions:

1. What are some ways people spend their vacation?

____

2. Why did Mary enjoy her vacation?

____

3. Why are community centers, like the YMCA, important?

____

4. Why might John have joined the basketball league?

____

5. How are traveling and sports activities different ways to enjoy free time?

____

6. What is the author's point of view on leisurely activities?

____

Exercise 3- Read the text below before answering the questions.

Relaxation and Exercise

Gyms are one of the most common facilities used during leisure time. People visit gyms to exercise, build strength, and stay healthy. Anna has membership at her local gym, and she visits three times a week. She believes regular exercise helps her relieve stress after work.

Another well-known facility is the YMCA, which offers different activities for both children and adults. The YMCA provides swimming lessons, fitness classes, and community events. Families enjoy going to the YMCA to stay active and spend quality time together.

Public parks are also popular leisure facilities. They provide space for jogging, family picnics, and playing sports. These parks are often visited during weekends when people want to spend time outdoors. The government ensures these parks are clean and safe for everyone to use.

Comprehension Questions:

1. What types of activities do people use gyms for?

   ____

2. Why does Anna visit her gym regularly?

   ____

3. What can we infer about the YMCA's role in the community?

   ____

4. What might be the purpose of offering family activities at the YMCA?

   ____

5. How are gyms and public parks different in the services they offer?

   ____

6. What is the author's view on the importance of public parks?

   ____

Exercise 4- Read the community facilities below before answering the questions.

Community Facilities

Agency	Service Provided	Contact Method	Operating Hours	Location
YMCA	Fitness classes, swimming, events	Phone, In-person	7 AM - 9 PM	Various locations
Community Park	Jogging, picnics, sports fields	No contact needed	6 AM - 10 PM	Local neighborhood
Public Library	Reading programs, workshops	Phone, In-person	9 AM - 5 PM	Main Street
Recreation Center	Indoor sports, gym facilities, workout classes	In-person	8 AM - 8 PM	City Center
Art Center	Art classes, exhibitions	Phone, Online	10 AM - 6 PM	Downtown

Comprehension Questions:

1. Which community agency offers swimming lessons?

   ____

2. What activities can people do at the community park?

   ____

3. Why do you think the YMCA provides different activities for families?

   ____

4. What might be the purpose of having art exhibitions at the Art Center?

   ____

5. How are the services of the YMCA and the Recreation Center similar?

   ____

6. What is the author's point of view on the importance of public libraries?

   ____

Exercise 5- Fill in the blanks with the correct words: *coach, gym, vacation, YMCA, membership* and *leisure.*

1. Many people use the _________________________________ to exercise and stay healthy.

2. The _________________________________ offers activities for both children and adults.

3. _________________________________ time is important for rest and relaxation.

4. John got _________________________________ at the community YMCA.

5. A _________________________________ helps athletes improve their skills.

6. Anna took a _________________________________ to relax after a busy year.

Exercise 6- Writing

Write a paragraph to summarize what you know and learned about leisure time activities and facilities in your own words.

ANSWER KEYS

Exercise 1- Vocabulary Matching:
1. Gym - f. A place to exercise
2. Vacation - d. A period of rest or travel
3. Facility - h. A building or place that provides a service
4. YMCA - e. A community center offering activities
5. Membership - a. The act of joining a club or organization
6. Sports - g. Physical games or activities
7. Coach - b. Someone who trains athletes
8. Leisure - c. Free time for relaxation

Exercise 2- Text 1:
1. People spend their vacations traveling, relaxing, or participating in sports.
2. She enjoyed it because she spent time reading on the beach and enjoying the sunny weather.
3. Community centers provide opportunities to stay active and meet people.
4. He wanted to improve his skills and meet new friends.
5. Traveling allows relaxation, while sports involve physical activity.
6. The author thinks leisurely activities are fun and great ways to stay healthy and connected with other people.

Exercise 3- Text 2:
1. People use gyms for exercise, building strength, and staying healthy.
2. Anna believes regular exercise helps her relieve stress.

3. The YMCA plays an important role by offering various activities for all ages.
4. The purpose is to help families stay active and spend quality time together.
5. Gyms are focused on indoor activities, while public parks offer broader outdoor activities.
6. The author views public parks as clean and safe spaces for people to relax and exercise.

Exercise 4- Community Facilities:
1. The YMCA offers swimming lessons.
2. People can jog, have picnics, and play sports at the community park.
3. The YMCA provides different activities for families to help them stay active and spend time together.
4. The purpose of having art exhibitions is to showcase artwork and offer a space for people to appreciate art.
5. They both offer fitness classes and other fitness-related activities.
6. The author seems to think they are important because they include the public library in the list of community facilities and state that they offer reading programs and workshops.

Exercise 5- Fill-in-the-Blanks:
1. gym
2. YMCA
3. leisure
4. membership
5. coach
6. vacation

Lesson 3: The U.S. Educational System

Objectives:

1. Students will read and answer questions about the educational system structure in the United States, including K-12 and community colleges.
2. Students will use new words to complete exercises related to accessing educational services and enrolling in different types of schools.

Exercise 1- Draw a line connecting each word to its correct definition.

Word	Meaning
1. Enrollment	a. A certificate received after finishing high school
2. Curriculum	b. Kindergarten through 12th grade
3. Community College	c. A person who gives advice
4. Elementary School	d. The fee paid to attend school
5. Diploma	e. The subjects taught in school
6. Tuition	f. The first years of schooling for children
7. Counselor	g. A local school for adults
8. K-12	h. The process of signing up for school

Exercise 2- Read the text below before answering the questions.

Understanding the K-12 System

The K-12 educational system in the United States includes kindergarten through 12th grade. K-12 education is an important foundation for a student's success in life. This system provides free public education for children, starting at age five or six. The main purpose of K-12 is to prepare students for higher education or careers after high school. Elementary school is the first stage, followed by middle school, and then high school.

High schools offer a variety of subjects, such as mathematics, science, and arts. Students can also participate in extracurricular activities like sports and music. Maria enrolled her daughter in high school last year, and she is now enjoying both her classes and playing on the school soccer team.

Comprehension Questions:

1. What does the K-12 system include?

____

2. Why is K-12 education provided?

____

3. What do you think is the importance of extracurricular activities in high schools?

____

4. How does high school differ from elementary school?

____

5. Why does the author mention that Maria's daughter is enjoying high school?

____

6. What is the author's view on K-12 education?

____

Exercise 3- Read the text below before answering the questions.

Community College

Community colleges provide opportunities for adults to continue their education. These colleges are usually more affordable compared to universities. They are also more flexible, meaning students can choose classes that fit their schedules, such as evening or weekend classes. They offer a variety of programs, including certificates and associate degrees. James decided to enroll in a community college to study computer science while working part-time.

In addition to academic courses, community colleges also provide services such as counseling and job placement. Students are encouraged to use these services to plan their education and career paths. The counselor at James' community college helped him decide which courses would be best for his career goals.

Comprehension Questions:

1. What kind of opportunities do community colleges provide?

____

2. Why did James enroll in community college?

____

3. What do you think are the benefits of counseling services at community colleges?

____

4. How is community college different from universities?

____

5. Why does the author explain that community colleges offer flexible schedules for students?

____

6. What is the author's view on the value of community college services?

____

Exercise 4- Read the registration information below before answering the questions.

Registration Information

Level	Age Group	Registration Process	Duration	Cost (Typical)
Pre-K	4-5 years	Local application required	1 year	free (in some states)
Elementary School	5-11 years	Automatic district enrollment	6 years	Free
Middle School	11-14 years	Automatic district enrollment	3 years	Free
High School	14-18 years	Automatic district enrollment	4 years	Free
Community College	18+ years	Application online or in-person	2-3 years	Tuition applies (varies)

Comprehension Questions:

1. What is the typical age for enrollment in elementary school?

____

2. What is the registration process for pre-k?

____

3. Why do you think free public education is offered for K-12 students?

____

4. How does the registration process for high school differ from that of community college?

____

5. Why does the author mention that community colleges require tuition?

____

6. Why do you think the author includes the duration of each level in the table?

____

Exercise 5- Fill in the blanks with the correct words: curriculum, diploma, tuition, enrollment, community college and counselor

1. To attend __________________________________, students must fill out an application.

2. The ____________________________ includes subjects like math, science, and arts.

3. ____________________________ is the process of signing up for classes.

4. High school students receive a ____________________________when they graduate.

5. The ____________________________ helps students plan their courses.

6. ____________________________ is the fee paid for classes at a college.

Exercise 6- Writing

Write a paragraph to summarize what you know and learned about the education system in your own words.

ANSWER KEYS

Exercise 1- Vocabulary Matching:

- Enrollment - h. The process of signing up for school
- Curriculum - e. The subjects taught in school
- Community College - g. A local school for adults
- Elementary School - f. the first years of schooling for children
- Diploma - a. A certificate received after finishing high school
- Tuition - d. The fee paid to attend school
- Counselor - c. A person who gives advice
- K-12 - b. Kindergarten through 12th grade

Exercise 2- Text 1:

1. The K-12 system includes kindergarten through 12th grade.
2. The purpose is to prepare students for higher education or careers.
3. Extracurricular activities help students enjoy school, gain new skills and make friends.
4. High school offers more advanced subjects and extracurricular activities.
5. The author mentions Maria's daughter enjoying high school to show that high school can be enjoyable with both learning and fun activities.
6. The author views it as very important, calling it one of the most important foundations for a student's success.

Exercise 3- Text 2:

1. Community colleges provide opportunities for adults to continue their education.
2. He wanted to study computer science while working part-time.
3. Counseling services help students choose the best courses for their careers.
4. Community colleges are more affordable and flexible compared to universities.
5. The author does this to show that they are good options for adults who need to work and study.
6. The author thinks community college services are important for students to plan their education and career.

Exercise 4- Registration Information:

1. The typical age is between 5 and 11 years old.
2. The registration process requires a local application to be submitted.
3. Free public education is offered to ensure that all children have the opportunity to receive an education, regardless of their families' financial situations.
4. The registration process for high school is automatic through district enrollment, while community college requires students to apply either online or in person.
5. The author mentions that community colleges require tuition so the readers will know that higher education comes with a cost.
6. The author includes the duration to help readers see how long each stage of education lasts and understand the time needed for each level.

Exercise 5- Fill-in-the-Blanks:

1. community college
2. curriculum
3. enrollment
4. diploma
5. counselor
6. tuition

REFLECTION ON LEARNING

Answer the following questions and discuss your responses with your teacher or classmates.

1. What reading strategies did you learn or practice in this unit?

2. What new concepts or words did you learn?

3. What reading challenges did you face?

4. What reading strategies do you need to improve?

5. What do you want your teacher to know?

Lesson 1: Medical Specialists and Insurance

Objectives:

1. Students will read and answer questions on healthcare, the roles of medical specialists, and medical insurance.
2. Students will use new words to complete exercises about healthcare, medical specialists and insurance.

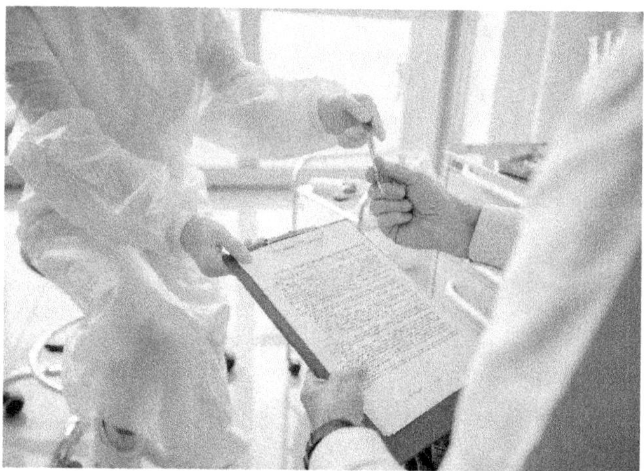

Exercise 1- Draw a line connecting each word to its correct definition.

Word	Meaning
1. Specialist	a. Care or medication to improve your health
2. Primary care provider (PCP)	b. The doctor's finding about a condition
3. Appointment	c. A main doctor who helps with general health
4. Insurance	d. A plan of care or appointments
5. Schedule	e. A visit to the doctor to assess your health
6. Diagnosis	f. A doctor who focuses on a specific area of health
7. Treatment	g. A set time to meet with a doctor
8. Examination	h. Financial protection for health costs

Comprehension Questions:

1. What types of specialists are listed in the table?

   ____

2. Which specialist accepts all insurance types?

   ____

3. On which days can you schedule an appointment with a cardiologist?

   ____

4. What is the room number for the dermatologist?

   ____

5. Which doctors serve as PCPs?

   ____

6. How does the schedule for the pediatrician compare to that of the general surgeon?

   ____

Exercise 5- Fill in the blanks with the correct words: treatment, specialist, insurance, examination, appointment and diagnosis.

1. A referral from a primary care provider is needed to see a _______________________.

2. An _______________________ plan helps you lower your medical costs.

3. The _______________________ determines what medication is needed.

4. You need to make an _______________________ to see your doctor for a check-up.

5. It's important to follow the _______________________ your doctor recommends.

6. Many people have an annual health _______________________.

Exercise 6- Writing

Write a paragraph to summarize what you know and learned about medical practitioners and insurance.

ANSWER KEYS

Exercise 1- Vocabulary Matching:
1. Specialist - f. A doctor who focuses on a specific area of health
2. Primary care provider (PCP) - c. A main doctor who helps with general health
3. Appointment - g. A set time to meet with a doctor
4. Insurance - h. Financial protection for health costs
5. Schedule - d. A plan of care or appointments
6. Diagnosis - b. The doctor's finding about a condition
7. Treatment – a. Care or medication to improve your health
8. Examination - e. A visit to the doctor to assess your health

Exercise 2- Text 1:
1. The passage explains the importance of regular check-ups, primary care providers, and insurance.
2. A PCP provides general health care and helps prevent sickness.
3. Insurance helps by covering part of the costs of healthcare services.
4. Routine examination may include physical checks, health history, and recommendations.
5. A PCP provides general health care, helps prevent illness, and connects you to specialists.
6. Insurance lowers the costs of appointments and treatments, making healthcare more affordable.

Exercise 3- Text 2:
1. The passage explains the importance of understanding medical insurance and specialist care.
2. Insurance might cover doctor visits, hospital stays, medication, and specialist care.
3. They might need a referral to ensure that they see the right specialist for their specific health issue.
4. A specialist focuses on specific areas of medicine, while a PCP offers general care.
5. It is important to know so patients can avoid unexpected expenses and afford necessary care.
6. The author believes understanding insurance coverage is essential for making informed decisions about healthcare.

Exercise 4- Medical Specialists Information:
1. The specialists are a cardiologist, dermatologist, general surgeon, pediatrician, and family doctor.
2. The general surgeon and the family doctor accept all types of insurance.
3. You can schedule an appointment with a cardiologist on Monday, Wednesday, and Friday.
4. The room number for the dermatologist is Room 210.
5. The pediatrician and the family doctor serve as PCPs.
6. The pediatrician is available every weekday from Monday to Friday, while the general surgeon is only available on Monday, Tuesday, and Friday.

Exercise 5- Fill-in-the-Blanks:
1. specialist
2. insurance
3. diagnosis
4. appointment
5. treatment
6. examination

Healthcare in the U.S. can be expensive, so people often use health insurance. Insurance helps pay for doctor visits, treatments, and medication. Without insurance, the cost can be very high. James uses his insurance to cover most of his medical expenses, including doctor visits and prescriptions.

Comprehension Questions:

1. What do patients do after getting a prescription?

____

2. Why is health insurance important?

____

3. What role does insurance play in medical expenses?

____

4. How is prescription medication different from over-the-counter medication?

____

5. Why did James go to his local pharmacy?

____

6. What is the author's view on using insurance for healthcare?

____

Exercise 4- Read the healthcare information below before answering the questions.

Healthcare Information

Facility Type	Description	Services Provided	Typical Hours
Drugstore	Store for medicine and health products	Over-the-counter drugs, prescriptions	9 AM - 9 PM
Clinic	Local medical care facility	Check-ups, minor treatments	8 AM - 6 PM
Dentist Office	Dental health services	Cleanings, fillings, braces	9 AM - 5 PM
Doctor's Office	General health care provider	Check-ups, diagnosis, referrals	8 AM - 5 PM

Comprehension Questions:

1. What type of services are provided by a drugstore?

____

2. When can you visit a clinic for medical care?

____

3. What do the clinic's opening hours suggest about the type of care it provides?

____

4. How is a drugstore different from a clinic in the services provided?

____

5. What is the purpose of a dentist's office?

____

6. Why do you think the author included the operating hours of each facility?

____

Exercise 5- Fill in the blanks with the correct words: insurance, appointment, hospital, clinic, pharmacy and prescription.

1. To see a doctor, you must schedule an ________________________________

2. A ________________________________ sells medications prescribed by doctors.

3. ________________________________ helps pay for medical costs, like doctor visits and medications.

4. A ________________________________ is a place where you can get treated for minor illnesses.

5. A ________________________________ from a doctor is needed to buy certain types of medication.

6. An emergency requires urgent care at a ________________________________.

Exercise 6- Writing

Write a paragraph to summarize what you know and learned about the healthcare system in your own words.

ANSWER KEYS

Exercise 1- Vocabulary Matching:
1. Hospital - A building where people go when they are very sick, injured, or need surgery
2. Pharmacy - A store where medications are sold
3. Insurance - A plan that helps pay for medical expenses
4. Clinic - A place where people receive medical care or check-ups
5. Prescription - A written order from a doctor for medication
6. Specialist - A doctor who is an expert in a particular area
7. Emergency - A serious and urgent situation
8. Referral - A note from a doctor to see a specialist

Exercise 2- Text 1:
1. The healthcare system offers services such as clinics, hospitals, and specialists.
2. People visit clinics because they provide services like routine check-ups and treatment for minor illnesses.
3. Scheduling an appointment helps ensure that patients are seen by the doctor at a specific time.
4. Clinics offer routine check-ups and minor care, while hospitals handle emergencies and surgeries.
5. Maria visited a specialist for her back pain after her primary doctor referred her.
6. The author thinks clinics make non-emergency care easily accessible.

Exercise 3- Text 2:
1. Patients take the prescription to the pharmacy to get their medication.
2. Health insurance is important because it helps pay for healthcare services.
3. Insurance helps people manage the high costs of medical treatment.
4. Prescription medication requires a doctor's approval, unlike over-the-counter drugs.
5. James went to his pharmacy to get his allergy medication.
6. The author believes insurance plays a crucial role in making healthcare affordable.

Exercise 4- Healthcare Information:
1. A drugstore provides over-the-counter drugs and prescriptions.
2. You can visit a clinic for medical care from 8 AM to 6 PM.
3. The clinic's opening hours suggest that it provides non-emergency care, such as check-ups and minor treatments, rather than emergency care.
4. A drugstore provides medications (over-the-counter drugs and prescriptions), while a clinic provides medical care services like check-ups and minor treatments.
5. The purpose of a dentist's office is to provide dental health services, such as cleanings, fillings, and braces.
6. The author included the operating hours to help readers understand when each facility is available, so they can choose the best option based on their needs and schedule.

Exercise 5- Fill-in-the-Blanks:
1. appointment
2. pharmacy
3. insurance
4. clinic
5. prescription
6. hospital

Lesson 3- Healthcare and Medical Forms

Objectives:

1. Students will read and answer questions on different types of healthcare forms and how to fill them out correctly.
2. Students will use new words to complete exercises related to healthcare forms and understand the purpose of each form.

Word	Meaning
1. Consent	a. The kind of medical costs your insurance will help pay for
2. Insurance provider	b. A number on your insurance card that shows it belongs to you
3. Specialized treatment	c. Signs of illness
4. Coverage type	d. Special treatment from a doctor who focuses on one area of health
5. Medical History	e. The process of asking for payment
6. Billing	f. A record of past health issues
7. Symptoms	g. Permission for something to happen
8. Policy number	h. The company that gives you health insurance to help pay for medical costs

Types of Healthcare Forms

Healthcare forms play a vital role in the medical system. Patients are often asked to fill out different forms before they receive any treatment. A common type of form is the consent form, which gives permission to doctors to carry out certain treatments or tests. This form ensures that the patient understands what procedures will be done.

Another important form is the medical history form. This form records the patient's past illnesses, surgeries, and family history of diseases. Maria, for instance, had to fill out a medical history form when she went for a check-up at her local clinic. The information provided on this form helps doctors make diagnoses and informed decisions about the best course of treatment.

Comprehension Questions:

1. What is the purpose of a consent form?

____

2. Why are patients asked to fill out a medical history form?

____

3. Why is it important for patients to give consent before receiving treatment?

____

4. How are consent forms different from medical history forms?

____

5. Why does the author include the example of Maria filling out a medical history form?

____

6. What is the author's view on the importance of healthcare forms?

____

Healthcare Insurance and Referral Forms

Healthcare insurance forms are essential for covering medical costs. Insurance helps protect patients from high medical expenses. Before receiving treatment, patients must provide information about their insurance plan. This is often done through a form called the insurance claim form. Katie Wright filled out an insurance form before her doctor's appointment to cover the cost of her examination.

Another form commonly used is the referral form. A referral form is used when a patient needs to see a specialist. Peter Hegel, for example, received a referral from his doctor to see a dentist. Referral forms make it easier for patients to get specialized care that is beyond the primary doctor's expertise.

Comprehension Questions:

1. What is the purpose of an insurance form?

____

2. How does insurance protect patients?

____

3. Why are referral forms important, based on the information given in the passage?

____

4. How are insurance forms different from referral forms?

____

5. Why does the author describe how referral forms get patients specialized care?

____

6. What is the author's view on the role of referral forms?

____

Exercise 4- Read the form below before answering the questions.

Dental Examination Form for Peter Hegel

Form Field	Value
Patient Name	Peter Hegel
Appointment Date	12/10/2024
Type of Examination	Dental Check-Up
Dentist's Name	Dr. Simmons
Comments	Routine examination, no issues found

Comprehension Questions:

1. Who is the patient for this dental examination?

____

2. When is Peter's appointment?

____

3. What can we understand about Peter's health based on the comments?

____

4. How is this form different from a medical examination form?

____

5. Why is there a section for the dentist's comments?

____

Exercise 5- Read the form below before answering the questions.

Medical Examination Form for Maria Diallo

Form Field	Value
Patient Name	Maria Diallo
Appointment Date	15/10/2024
Type of Examination	General Check-Up
Doctor's Name	Dr. Lee
Medical History Noted	High blood pressure

Comprehension Questions:

1. What is the purpose of this medical examination form?

____

2. What medical issue is noted for Maria?

____

3. Why do you think Maria is having a general check-up?

____

4. How does this form compare to the dental examination form?

____

5. What is Dr. Lee's role in this examination?

____

Health Insurance Form for Katie Wright:

Form Field	Value
Patient's Name	Katie Wright
Insurance Provider	HealthFirst
Policy Number	HF-123456
Coverage Type	General Health
Expiration Date	2/10/2027

Comprehension Questions:

1. What type of form is being presented?

____

2. What is Katie's insurance provider?

____

3. Why is the type of coverage included in the form?

____

4. How is an insurance form different from a medical examination form?

____

5. Why is it important to give the correct information on these kinds of forms?

____

Exercise 7- Fill in the blanks with the correct words: *billing, coverage, consent, insurance provider* and *referral.*

1. Patients must fill out a _______________________________ form before receiving treatment.

2. Katie's _____________________, HealthFirst, helps cover the cost of her medical expenses.

3. A _______________________________ form includes information about past illnesses.

4. A _______________________________ form is used to see a specialist.

5. _______________________________ is the process of asking for payment for healthcare services.

6. My health insurance provides _______________________________ for doctor visits and hospital stays.

Exercise 8- Writing

Write a paragraph to summarize what you know and learned about medical forms in your own words.

ANSWER KEYS

Exercise 1- Vocabulary Matching:
1. Consent - g. Permission for something to happen
2. Insurance provider - h. The company that gives you health insurance to help pay for medical costs
3. Specialized treatment - d. Special treatment from a doctor who focuses on one area of health
4. Coverage type - a. The kind of medical costs your insurance will help pay for
5. Medical History - f. A record of past health issues
6. Billing - e. The process of asking for payment
7. Symptoms - c. Signs of illness
8. Policy number - b. A number on your insurance card that shows it belongs to you

Exercise 2- Text 1:
1. The purpose of a consent form is to give doctors permission to perform treatments and tests.
2. Patients fill out a medical history form so that doctors can make decisions about diagnoses and treatment.
3. It is important for patients to give consent because it shows they understand the treatment

specialized care they need.

Exercise 4- Dental Examination Form for Peter Hegel:
1. The patient for this dental examination is Peter Hegel.
2. Peter's appointment is on 12/10/2024.
3. We can understand that Peter's health is good, as the examination was routine and no issues were found.
4. This form is specific to a dental check-up, while a medical examination form would be used for a general health check-up.
5. The section allows the dentist to provide important details about the examination, such as any observations or findings.

Exercise 5- Medical Examination Form for Maria Diallo:
1. This form is used to collect information about the patient's health, the doctor, and the reason for the check-up.
2. Maria has high blood pressure.
3. Maria is having a general check-up to check her overall health and monitor her high blood pressure.
4. This form is for a general health check, while the dental form is for checking teeth and gums.

or test they will receive and agree to it. This helps protect both the patient and the doctor.

4. Consent forms are for permission, while medical history forms record past illnesses.

5. The author includes the example to show how this form is used in real-life situations and to help readers understand its importance.

6. The author believes healthcare forms are vital in the medical system as they help doctors understand patient needs.

Exercise 3- Text 2:

1. The insurance form is used to cover medical costs.

2. Insurance helps protect patients by reducing their medical expenses.

3. Referral forms help patients access specialized care.

4. Insurance forms provide coverage details, while referral forms direct patients to specialists.

5. The author includes this description to explain the benefits of referral forms and how they ensure patients receive care for their specific health needs.

6. The author views referral forms as an important part of helping patients receive the

5. Dr. Lee is the doctor who will check Maria's health and give advice or treatment.

Exercise 6- Health Insurance Form for Katie Wright:

1. It is a health insurance form.

2. Katie's insurance provider is HealthFirst.

3. This is included to show the kind of medical expenses the insurance will cover, so the patient will know what they will need to pay for themselves.

4. An insurance form includes details about the patient's insurance, while a medical examination form focuses on the patient's medical history,

5. It is important so the insurance can pay for your medical care without any problems. This helps make sure you get the right treatment on time.

Exercise 7- Fill-in-the-Blanks:

1. consent
2. insurance provider
3. medical history
4. referral
5. billing
6. coverage

Lesson 4: Medications

Objectives:

1. Students will read and answer questions on choosing and using medications safely.
2. Students will use new words to complete exercises on medication labels and instructions.

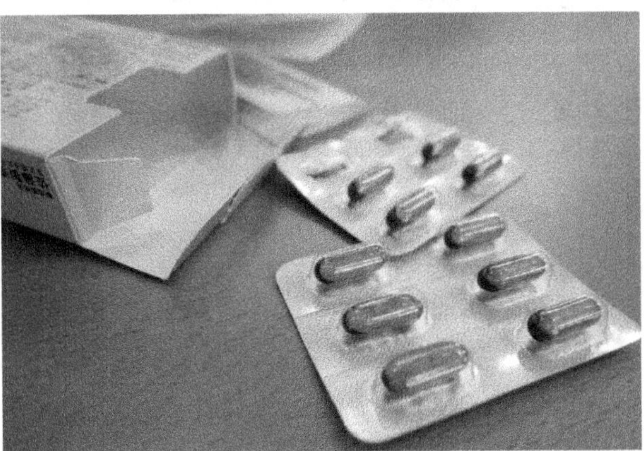

Exercise 1- Draw a line connecting each word to its correct definition.

Word	Meaning
1. Dosage	a. Caution or advice about risks
2. Prescription	b. A substance used to treat illness
3. Side Effect	c. The amount of medicine to take
4. Warning	d. Signs of illness
5. Medication	e. Doctor's written order for medicine
6. Over-the-Counter	f. A medicine store
7. Pharmacy	g. An unintended reaction from medicine
8. Symptoms	h. Available without prescription

Exercise 2- Read the text below before answering the questions.

The Right Medication

In the United States, there are many types of medications available for different health issues. Some medications, called prescription drugs, require a doctor's approval. Others, known as over-the-counter (OTC) medications, can be purchased without a prescription. It's important to read the dosage instructions carefully to ensure safe use. For instance, cold medicines and pain relievers are often available OTC. However, each has specific directions on how much to take and how often.

When buying medication, always check the warning label. The warning label provides essential information, such as potential side effects and how it works with other drugs. Some common side effects of OTC medications include drowsiness and dry mouth. If you experience severe side effects, it's recommended to stop using the medication and consult a doctor.

Knowing where to buy medications is also important. You can find OTC medications at any pharmacy. If you need prescription drugs, you'll need a doctor's note, which the pharmacy will use to give you the correct medication. Following these steps ensures that you select and use medications safely.

Comprehension Questions:

1. What is the main idea of the text?

____

2. What is a prescription drug?

____

3. What is one common side effect of OTC medications?

____

4. Why is it important to read the warning label on medications?

____

5. Where can you buy over-the-counter medications?

____

6. What should you do if you experience severe side effects?

____

Exercise 3- Read the text below before answering the questions.

Dosage and Safety Tips

Every medication comes with a dosage instruction, which tells you how much medicine to take and how often. Following the correct dosage is essential for safety. If you take too little, the medication may not work. Taking too much can lead to an overdose, which can be dangerous. Always use the measuring device provided, such as a cup or spoon, to get the correct dosage.

In addition to dosage, it's essential to be aware of side effects. Some medications, like pain relievers, may cause stomach upset or dizziness. The warning label on the medication provides guidance, like not driving if the medicine causes drowsiness.

If you are unsure about any medication, ask the pharmacist for help. Pharmacists are trained to help you understand your medication, including dosage, side effects, and warnings. By taking these steps, you can safely use medications and avoid problems.

Comprehension Questions:

1. What is the main idea of the text?

____

2. Why is it important to follow the correct dosage?

____

3. What should you use to measure liquid medicine?

____

4. What might be a side effect of taking pain relievers?

____

5. Who can help if you have questions about a medicine?

____

6. What is one piece of advice given in the text for using medications safely?

____

Exercise 4- Read the medication information below before answering the questions.

Medication Information Table

Medication Type	Dosage	Side Effect	Warning
Pain Reliever	1 tablet	Drowsiness	Avoid driving.
Cough Syrup	2 teaspoons	Dizziness	Do not mix with alcohol.
Antibiotic	1 capsule	Stomach upset	Take it with food.
Allergy Medication	1 tablet	Dry mouth	Drink water.
Cold Medicine	1 dose cup	Sleepiness	Avoid heavy machinery.

Comprehension Questions:

1. What side effect is associated with pain relievers?

   ____

2. Why should you avoid alcohol when taking cough syrup?

   ____

3. How should antibiotics be taken to avoid stomach upset?

   ____

4. What is recommended when taking allergy medication?

   ____

5. What warning is given for cold medicine?

   ____

6. What might happen if you ignore the warning for pain relievers?

   ____

Exercise 5- Fill in the blanks with the correct words: *side effects, pharmacy, dosage, prescription, Symptoms,* and *consumer.*

1. Always check the _______________________ on the label to know how much medication to take.

2. A doctor's _______________________________ is required for certain drugs.

3. Be cautious of _______________________________ when starting new medication.

4. Over-the-counter medication can be bought at any _______________________________.

5. The _______________________________ label provides safety instructions and possible side effects.

6. Know the _______________________________ of an allergic reaction to medication.

Exercise 6- Writing

Write a paragraph to summarize what you know and learned about medication labels and instructions in your own words.

ANSWER KEYS

Exercise 1- Vocabulary Matching:

1. Dosage - c. The amount of medicine to take
2. Prescription - e. Doctor's written order for medicine
3. Side Effect - g. An unintended reaction from medicine
4. Warning - a. Caution or advice about risks
5. Medication - b. A substance used to treat illness
6. Over-the-Counter - h. Available without prescription
7. Pharmacy - f. A medicine store
8. Symptoms - d. Signs of illness

Exercise 2- Text 1:

1. The text explains how to choose and safely use different types of medications.
2. This is a medication that requires a doctor's approval to obtain.
3. Drowsiness is one common side effect.
4. It is important so you understand possible side effects and how the drug works with other medicines.
5. You can buy them at any pharmacy.
6. You should stop using the medication and consult a doctor.

Exercise 3- Text 2:

1. The main idea is to take medicine safely by following dosage instructions and safety tips.
2. It is important to ensure the medicine works and to avoid overdose.
3. You should use a measuring device provided, like a cup or spoon.
4. A side effect might be stomach upset or dizziness.
5. A pharmacist can help.
6. Always read the warning label for guidance on usage.

Exercise 4- Medication Information:

1. Drowsiness is associated with pain relievers.
2. It can increase dizziness.
3. They should be taken with food.
4. Drink water to prevent dry mouth.
5. Avoid operating heavy machinery.
6. There could be a risk of accidents due to drowsiness.

Exercise 5- Fill-in-the-Blanks:

1. Dosage
2. Prescription
3. Side effects
4. Pharmacy
5. Warning
6. Symptoms

REFLECTION ON LEARNING

Answer the following questions and discuss your responses with your teacher or classmates.

1. What reading strategies did you learn or practice in this unit?

2. What new concepts or words did you learn?

3. What reading challenges did you face?

4. What reading strategies do you need to improve?

5. What do you want your teacher to know?

Lesson 1: Getting a Job

Objectives:

1. Students will read and answer questions about the key methods and tools for job searching in the U.S.
2. Students will use new words to complete exercises about job application and interview techniques.

Exercise 1- Draw a line connecting each word to its correct definition.

Word	Meaning
1. Networking	a. Extra support or services provided by an employer
2. Job seeker	b. Regular payment for work
3. Recruiter	c. A document that lists your skills, work experience and education
4. Job Fair	d. An organization protecting worker rights
5. Resume	e. A person or company that helps find people for job positions
6. Benefits	f. A process of meeting people to share job opportunities
7. Salary	g. A person who is actively looking for work
8. Union	h. A public event to meet recruiters

Exercise 2- Read the text below before answering the questions.

Job Opportunities

Finding a job involves multiple strategies. One effective method is networking, where people connect and share information about job opportunities. Networking can happen at events, social gatherings, or through professional websites like LinkedIn. LinkedIn is a popular platform that helps professionals show their skills and experience. It also helps them connect with recruiters and colleagues.

Another way to search for jobs is through online job boards, such as Indeed, where employers post open positions. Job seekers can search for jobs by location, industry, and job type. Regularly updating one's resume and applying to positions on websites can increase the chances of finding a job. Job fairs are also an excellent opportunity to meet recruiters and learn more about companies hiring for different positions.

Comprehension Questions:

1. What is the main idea of the passage?

____

2. What is LinkedIn used for?

____

3. How does Indeed help in job searching?

____

4. Why is networking important in the job search process?

____

5. How do job fairs assist job seekers?

____

6. What is the author's view on using online platforms for job searching?

____

Exercise 3- Read the text below before answering the questions.

Job Application

When looking at job postings, it's essential to understand the requirements and benefits of the position. Job postings often tell you the requirements, such as specific skills or years of experience, needed for the job. The salary or pay rate is also included, so job seekers know how much money they will earn.

Additionally, many job postings list benefits such as health insurance, paid vacation, and retirement plans. Some positions may require membership in a union. The union helps protect workers' rights and offers support. It is important to follow application instructions carefully, whether it's submitting a resume online or attending an in-person interview. This will help you make a good impression.

Comprehension Questions:

1. What information is typically included in a job posting?

____

2. Why are listing the requirements important?

____

3. What types of benefits might a job offer?

____

4. How does a union support workers?

____

5. What is the significance of including the salary in a job posting?

____

6. From the author's point of view, what will make a good impression?

____

Exercise 4- Read the job postings below before answering the questions.

Job Postings

Job Title	Eligibility	Salary	Benefits	Union	Application Instructions
Software Engineer	Bachelor's Degree	$80,000/year	Health, Dental, Retirement	No	Apply online.
Nurse	Nursing License	$70,000/year	Health, Retirement	Yes	Submit resume via website.
Teacher	Teaching Certificate	$50,000/year	Health, Paid Vacation	Yes	Send resume and cover letter.
Sales Associate	High School Diploma	$30,000/year	None	No	Walk-in interview
Electrician	Certification	$60,000/year	Health, Paid Leave	Yes	Apply via union website.

Comprehension Questions:

1. What is the salary for a software engineer?

____

2. Which job requires a high school diploma?

____

3. How does the sales associate apply for the position?

____

4. Which positions require union membership?

____

5. What benefits does a nurse receive?

____

6. Why might eligibility requirements vary for each position?

____

Exercise 5- Read the interview preparation techniques below before answering the questions.

Interview Preparation Techniques

Technique	Description
Research the company.	Learn about the company values and goals.
Prepare questions.	Have questions to ask the interviewer.
Practice common questions.	Practice answering typical interview questions.
Dress professionally.	Wear appropriate attire for the interview.
Arrive early.	Be punctual to make a good impression.
Bring extra copies.	Bring extra copies of your resume and cover letter.
Follow up.	Send a thank-you email after the interview.

Comprehension Questions:

1. Why is researching the company important?

____

2. What might happen if you arrive late to an interview?

____

3. Why should you bring extra copies of your resume?

____

4. How can following up after an interview help?

____

5. What is the purpose of dressing professionally?

____

6. How does practicing questions prepare you for an interview?

____

Exercise 6- Fill in the blanks with the correct words: *postings, networking, benefits, resumes, union,* and *application.*

1. LinkedIn is used for ______________________________.

2. Job ______________________________ often list requirements and benefits.

3. A ______________________________ helps protect workers' rights.

4. It's essential to follow ______________________________ instructions when applying.

5. Retirement plans and paid vacation are often listed as job ______________________________.

6. Job seekers should bring extra copies of their ______________________________ to interviews.

Exercise 7- Writing

Write a paragraph in your own words to summarize what you know and learned about getting a job.

ANSWER KEYS

Exercise 1- Vocabulary Matching:

1. Networking - f. A process of meeting people to share job opportunities
2. Job seeker - g. A person who is actively looking for work
3. Recruiter - e. A person or company that helps find people for job positions
4. Job Fair - h. A public event to meet recruiters
5. Resume - c. A document that lists your skills, work experience and education
6. Benefits - a. Extra support or services provided by an employer
7. Salary - b. Regular payment for work
8. Union - d. An organization protecting worker rights

Exercise 2- Text 1:

1. Networking and online platforms are key methods for job searching.
2. LinkedIn is used for professional networking online.
3. Indeed helps by providing job listings.
4. Networking helps people connect and share information about job opportunities, which can increase the chances of finding a job.
5. Job fairs allow job seekers to meet recruiters.
6. The author believes that applying to positions through online platforms can increase the chances of finding a job.

Exercise 3- Text 2:

1. Job postings usually include the job requirements, salary, and benefits.
2. It helps you know if you have the right skills or experience for the job.
3. A job might offer health insurance, paid vacation, and retirement plans.
4. A union helps protect workers' rights and gives support.
5. Including the salary in a job posting is important because it helps job seekers decide if the job meets their financial needs.

6. To make a good impression, the author states that you should follow the application instructions carefully.

Exercise 4- Job Posting:

1. The salary for a software engineer is $80,000 per year.
2. The sales associate position requires a high school diploma.
3. The sales associate applies for the position by attending a walk-in interview.
4. The nurse, teacher, and electrician positions require union membership.
5. A nurse receives health insurance and retirement benefits.
6. Eligibility requirements vary because each job requires different skills, qualifications, and levels of experience to perform the work effectively.

Exercise 5- Interview Preparation Techniques:

1. Researching the company is important because it shows you are interested and prepared.
2. If you arrive late, the interviewer might think you are irresponsible and cannot manage your time well.
3. You should bring extra copies in case the interviewer needs one.
4. Following up shows you are thankful and still interested in the job.
5. Dressing professionally shows that you respect the company and makes a good impression.
6. Practicing questions helps you feel ready and confident.

Exercise 6- Fill-in-the-Blanks:

1. networking
2. postings
3. union
4. application
5. benefits
6. resumes

Lesson 2: Wages, Benefits, and Employee Rights

Objectives:

1. Students will read and answer questions on wages, employee benefits, and rights in the U.S. workplace.
2. Students will use new words to complete exercises on employee protection, unions, and workplace fairness.

Exercise 1- Draw a line connecting each word to its correct definition.

Word	Meaning
1. Wages	a. Fair treatment in the workplace
2. Benefits	b. Harmful behavior between workers
3. Union	c. Money earned for working
4. Employee Rights	d. Monthly charge for membership
5. Membership Fee	e. Rules that ensure a fair work environment
6. Equal Opportunity	f. A group that supports employees through collective action
7. Complaint	g. Additional rewards from a job
8. Workplace Bullying	h. A reporting system for unfair treatment

Exercise 2- Read the text below before answering the questions.

Wages, Benefits, and Employee Rights in the U.S.

In the U.S., employees earn wages or salaries as compensation for their work. Wages are paid hourly, while salaries are fixed payments for a set period. Employees may also receive benefits, which can include health insurance, retirement plans, and paid vacation. Benefits add value to the job and provide financial security for employees.

Employee rights are essential to ensure all workers are treated fairly. These rights include protection from discrimination, equal opportunities to advance, and a safe work environment. Employers must follow laws that support these rights to maintain a fair workplace.

In cases of unfair treatment, employees can file complaints with Human Resources (HR) or other designated departments. This reporting system is vital for addressing issues and keeping the work environment healthy. It's essential for employees to be aware of their rights and the process of filing complaints to protect themselves and others.

Comprehension Questions:

1. What are the two types of compensation discussed in the text?

____

2. Why are benefits important for employees?

____

3. What is the main purpose of employee rights?

____

4. How can employees address unfair treatment?

____

5. Why is it essential for employees to know their rights?

____

6. What is the author's opinion on employee rights?

____

Exercise 3- Read the text below before answering the questions.

Union Organizations and Employee Protections

Union organizations provide support to employees through collective action. Unions negotiate for better wages, benefits, and working conditions on behalf of their members. Membership in a union often requires a monthly fee, known as a membership fee, which supports union activities and services.

One important aspect of union membership is the protection it offers against unfair treatment in the workplace. Union members have the right to participate in negotiations with employers. They also file complaints, known as grievances, if they feel mistreated. Unions play a crucial role in protecting employee rights and advocating for better working conditions.

Equal opportunity is strongly supported by unions. This means that all employees have the same chance for advancement and fair treatment regardless of their background. Unions often work with employers to promote equal opportunity, making the workplace more inclusive for all.

Comprehension Questions:

1. What is the main purpose of a union?

____

2. What is a membership fee used for?

____

3. How do unions support employee rights?

____

4. What role do unions play in promoting equal opportunities?

____

5. Why might an employee join a union?

____

6. What is the author's view on the importance of unions?

____

Exercise 4- Read the union organizations below before answering the questions.

Union Organizations

Union Organization	Benefits	Membership Fee
Service Employees International Union (SEIU)	Negotiates for healthcare and wage increases	$20/month
American Federation of Teachers (AFT)	Advocates for educational resources and fair wages	$25/month

Comprehension Questions:

1. What benefits does SEIU provide to its members?

____

2. What is the membership fee for the AFT?

____

3. How does the AFT support its members?

____

4. Which union might be more suitable for a teacher?

____

5. What is one main benefit of joining SEIU?

____

6. What does the membership fee support?

____

Exercise 5- Read the email below before answering the questions.

From:	hr@brightfuturetech.com
To:	employees@brightfuturetech.com
Subject:	Employee Rights and Reporting Procedures

Dear Employees,

We value each of you and are committed to maintaining a fair and respectful workplace. It is important for every employee to know their rights. As employees, you are entitled to fair treatment, protection from discrimination, and a safe working environment.

If you ever feel mistreated or experience discrimination, you can file an EEO (Equal Employment Opportunity) complaint with HR. Additionally, our workplace has a zero-tolerance policy for bullying. If you witness or experience bullying, report it immediately to HR. We want our workplace to be safe, respectful, and inclusive for everyone.

Sincerely,
Human Resources

Comprehension Questions:

1. What is the main purpose of the email?

____

2. What rights are employees entitled to?

____

3. What is an EEO complaint?

____

4. What is the policy on workplace bullying?

____

5. Who should employees contact if they experience bullying?

____

6. How does the email promote a respectful workplace?

____

Exercise 6- Fill in the blanks with the correct words: right, discrimination, complaint, bullying, membership fee, and union.

1. Employees should be protected from ____________________________ in the workplace.

2. A ____________________________ is a regular payment for union membership.

3. One purpose of a ____________________________ is to advocate for fair wages.

4. Employees have the ____________________________ to fair treatment in the workplace.

5. An EEO ____________________________ can be filed in cases of discrimination.

6. Workplace ____________________________ should be reported to HR immediately.

Exercise 7- Writing

Write three paragraphs in your own words to summarize what you know and learned about wages, employee benefits, and rights in the workplace.

ANSWER KEYS

Exercise 1- Vocabulary Matching:
1. Wages – c. Money earned for working
2. Benefits – g. Additional rewards from a job
3. Union – f. A group that supports employees through collective action
4. Employee Rights – e. Rules that ensure a fair work environment
5. Membership Fee - d. Monthly charge for membership
6. Equal Opportunity – a. Fair treatment in the workplace
7. Complaint – h. A reporting system for unfair treatment
8. Workplace Bullying – b. Harmful behavior between workers

Exercise 2- Text 1:
1. The two types of compensation are wages and salaries.
2. Benefits provide financial security and job value.
3. Employee rights ensure all workers are treated fairly.
4. Employees can file complaints with Human Resources (HR) or other designated departments.
5. Knowing their rights helps employees protect themselves and others.
6. The author believes that employee rights maintain a healthy and respectful work environment.

Exercise 3- Text 2:
1. A union supports employees by negotiating for better wages, benefits, and working conditions.
2. Membership fees fund union activities and services.
3. Unions negotiate for better wages and work conditions and help file grievances.
4. Unions ensure all employees have the same chance for advancement and fair treatment, regardless of their background.

5. An employee might join a union for protection against unfair treatment, to improve working conditions, and to have a voice in negotiations with employers.
6. The author views unions as essential for protecting workers' rights.

Exercise 4- Union Organizations:
1. SEIU provides healthcare and wage increase benefits.
2. AFT membership fee is $25/month.
3. AFT supports by advocating for resources and fair wages.
4. AFT is more suitable for a teacher.
5. Joining SEIU offers healthcare and wage support.
6. The membership fee funds union services and activities.

Exercise 5- HR email:
1. The purpose of the email is to inform employees of their rights and workplace policies.
2. Employees are entitled to fair treatment, discrimination protection, and a safe environment.
3. An EEO or Equal Employment complaint is when an employee tells HR about unfair treatment or discrimination.
4. The company has zero tolerance for bullying.
5. Employees should contact HR for bullying issues.
6. The email promotes respect by explaining employees' rights and how to report problems like bullying and discrimination.

Exercise 6- Fill-in-the-Blanks:
1. Discrimination
2. Membership Fee
3. Union
4. Right
5. Complaint
6. Bullying

Lesson 3: Job Performance and Training

Objectives:

1. Students will read and answer questions about job performance and training in the workplace.
2. Students will use new vocabulary to complete exercises about training materials and scheduling in a professional setting.

Exercise 1- Draw a line connecting each word to its correct definition.

Word	Meaning
1. Performance	a. Things you need to do your job well
2. Training	b. How well tasks are completed
3. Schedule	c. A letter for employees about training
4. Location	d. The place where training is held
5. HR Letter	e. Working on improving skills
6. Room Number	f. Happening every month
7. Skills	g. Time and day for training
8. Monthly	h. The number of the room for training

Exercise 2- Read the text below before answering the questions.

Job Performance and Training

Job performance is a key factor in career success. Employees are evaluated based on their ability to complete tasks well. Performance reviews often show strengths and the areas that need improvement. Consistent high performance can lead to career advancement.

Training is crucial for maintaining and improving job performance. Many companies offer various types of training, including technical skills, safety rules, and customer service. These programs help employees stay updated on industry standards and learn new skills. Regular training sessions support employees in achieving their career goals.

Monthly training schedules are common in many workplaces. Training can be mandatory or optional, depending on the job role. Employees are informed about training from HR. They get information on the dates, locations, and topics. Attending these sessions is often required to be ready for their jobs and follow company rules.

Comprehension Questions:

1. Why are performance reviews important?

____

2. How does training benefit employees?

____

3. What types of training might companies offer?

____

4. How are employees informed about training sessions?

____

5. Why might attendance at training sessions be mandatory?

____

6. What is the author's view on regular training?

____

Exercise 3- Read the text below before answering the questions.

Training Materials and Schedule

Training materials provide essential information for employees to succeed in their roles. These materials may include manuals, online resources, and hands-on activities. Each type of material offers a unique way to learn and improve skills relevant to the job.

Training sessions are scheduled so that most employees can attend. Companies often organize monthly or quarterly training sessions to ensure all team members have an opportunity to participate. Sessions may take place in different locations within the company, including training rooms, conference halls, or even virtual platforms.

HR plays an important role in communicating information on training. HR departments send out letters or emails informing employees about mandatory sessions, topics, and schedules. Regular updates from HR help employees stay prepared and meet job expectations. This system ensures everyone has the necessary resources for their roles.

Comprehension Questions:

1. What types of training materials are mentioned?

____

2. Why do companies hold regular training sessions?

____

3. Where can training sessions be held?

____

4. How does HR communicate training requirements?

____

5. Why is it important for employees to stay updated with training?

____

6. What is the author's opinion on HR's role in training?

____

Exercise 4- Read the training schedule below before answering the questions.

Training Schedule

Training Topic	Schedule	Location	Room Number
EEO Compliance	1st Monday, 10 AM	Training Room A	101
IT Security	2nd Wednesday, 2 PM	Conference Room B	202
Safety Protocol	3rd Friday, 9 AM	Training Room C	303
Customer Service	4th Thursday, 1 PM	Virtual	N/A
Leadership Skills	Last Monday, 11 AM	Conference Room D	404

Comprehension Questions:

1. When is the IT Security training scheduled?

____

2. Where does the Safety Protocol training take place?

____

3. What is the room number for the EEO Compliance training?

____

4. Which training session is held virtually?

____

5. Who might attend the Leadership Skills training?

____

6. How often are these training sessions held?

____

Exercise 5- Read the email below before answering the questions.

From:	hr@utdgroup.com
To:	employees@utdgroup.com
Subject:	Mandatory Training Sessions for This Month

Dear Employees,

To ensure we maintain a high standard of performance, we have scheduled mandatory training sessions this month. These sessions cover important topics such as Equal Employment Opportunity (EEO), IT security, and safety protocols. Attendance is required for all employees.

Each training session has been designed to support you in meeting job requirements and maintaining a safe and inclusive workplace. Please review the schedule provided and make arrangements to attend. If you have any questions, feel free to contact the HR department. Thank you for your commitment to excellence.

Sincerely,
Human Resources

Comprehension Questions:

1. What is the purpose of the email?

____

2. Which topics will the training sessions cover?

____

3. Who is required to attend the training sessions?

____

4. Why is it important for employees to attend?

____

5. How can employees get additional information?

____

6. What is HR's goal in organizing these sessions?

____

Exercise 6- Fill in the blanks with the correct words: email, room number, training, schedule, performance, and location.

1. HR sends an _______________________________ to employees about training requirements.

2. The _______________________________ for the customer service training is Virtual Room C.

3. _______________________________ sessions help improve job skills.

4. Employees can check the _______________________________ to find the training date.

5. Monthly training is part of the company's plan to improve employee _______________________.

6. The _______________________________ for the EEO training is 101.

Exercise 7- Writing

Write two paragraphs to summarize what you know and learned about job performance and training in your own words.

ANSWER KEYS

Exercise 1- Vocabulary Matching:
1. Performance - b. How well tasks are completed
2. Training - e. Working on improving skills
3. Schedule - g. Time and day for training
4. Location - d. The place where training is held
5. HR Letter - c. A letter for employees about training
6. Room Number - h. The number of the room for training
7. Skills - a. Things you need to do your job well
8. Monthly - f. Happening every month

Exercise 2- Text 1:
1. Performance reviews help employees recognize their strengths and weaknesses.
2. Training helps employees stay updated and learn new skills.
3. Companies may offer training in technical skills, safety rules, and customer service.
4. HR informs employees about training schedules.
5. Attendance might be mandatory to ensure employees are ready for their jobs and follow company rules.
6. The author believes regular training is important because it supports employees in achieving their career goals and improving their job performance.

Exercise 3- Text 2:
1. Training materials include manuals, online resources, and hands-on activities
2. Companies do this to ensure that all employees have an opportunity to attend and stay updated.
3. Sessions can be held in training rooms, conference halls, or virtual platforms.
4. HR sends emails and letters about training.
5. It is important so they can meet job expectations and have the necessary resources for their roles.
6. The author believes that HR plays an important role in providing employees with information and resources to succeed in their training.

Exercise 4- Text 3:
1. IT Security training is on the 2nd Wednesday at 2 PM.
2. Safety Protocol training is in Training Room C.
3. The room number for the EEO Compliance training is 101.
4. The Customer Service training is held virtually.
5. The Leadership Skills training may suit supervisors or managers.
6. The sessions are held monthly.

Exercise 5- HR Email:
1. The purpose of the email is to inform employees of mandatory training.
2. The training sessions will cover EEO, IT security, and safety protocols.
3. All employees must attend.
4. Employees must attend to meet job requirements and keep the workplace safe.
5. Employees can contact the HR department for more information.
6. HR wants to help employees meet job standards and keep the workplace safe.

Exercise 6- Fill-in-the-Blanks
1. email
2. location
3. training
4. schedule
5. performance
6. room number

Lesson 4: Workplace Communication

Objectives:

1. Students will read and answer questions about key communication strategies for professional settings.
2. Students will use new words to complete exercises on different communication methods like face-to-face, email, and virtual platforms.

Exercise 1- Draw a line connecting each word to its correct definition.

Word	Meaning
1. Communication	a. A process of assessing performance
2. Strategy	b. The exchange of information between people
3. Evaluation	c. The attitude or feeling shown in communication
4. Feedback	d. A gathering of people to discuss topics
5. Meeting	e. Guidance for improvement
6. Face-to-Face	f. An online video platform
7. Zoom	g. In-person interaction
8. Tone	h. A technique to achieve success

Communication at Work

In the modern workplace, communication is essential for achieving goals and building relationships. Face-to-face communication allows employees to read body language and express ideas clearly. This method is best for discussions that need immediate feedback or deal with complex topics. However, face-to-face communication may not always be possible, especially in remote or hybrid work environments.

Email communication is another popular method in the workplace. It is suitable for sending detailed information, instructions, or follow-ups. Emails are useful because they keep a written record of what was said. However, while emails are efficient, they may lack the personal touch of face-to-face communication. They may then lead to misunderstandings because they do not show tone or emotion.

Zoom and other online platforms have become common in the workplace. These tools allow teams to have virtual meetings and communicate even from different locations. Zoom combines the benefits of both face-to-face and written communication. It allows people to see each other and keeps a record of meeting minutes. It is a useful tool for companies with remote employees or global teams.

Comprehension Questions:

1. What are the benefits of face-to-face communication?

____

2. Why might email lead to misunderstandings?

____

3. When is Zoom particularly useful in a workplace setting?

____

4. How can emails be useful in communication?

____

5. What is the main idea of the text?

____

6. What is the author's view on Zoom as a tool for remote teams?

____

Effective Communication Strategies

Effective communication strategies are essential for workplace success. Active listening helps employees understand each other better, reduces misunderstandings, and builds trust. It includes asking questions and paying attention to show interest, which helps teams work better together.

Providing clear feedback is another important strategy. Constructive feedback supports personal and professional growth. Employees who receive regular feedback are more likely to feel valued and motivated. HR departments often organize sessions to train employees to give and receive feedback effectively.

Another useful strategy is changing tone depending on the situation. Professional communication should always be respectful and clear. When communicating in writing, avoid ambiguous language so others do not misunderstand. This approach is especially relevant when communicating through email or reports where tone can be easily misunderstood.

Comprehension Questions:

1. Why is active listening important in the workplace?

____

2. How does feedback help employees?

____

3. What does HR do to support effective communication?

____

4. Why should written communication avoid ambiguous language?

____

5. What is the main purpose of changing tone according to the situation?

____

6. What is the author's opinion on the importance of feedback?

____

Workplace Communication Strategies

Strategies	Description
Active Listening	Paying full attention to the speaker
Providing Feedback	Offering constructive criticism
Adapting Tone	Changing the communication style based on the situation
Body Language	Using gestures to support spoken words
Asking Questions	Engaging others to understand better
Being Clear	Using simple and direct language
Respecting Boundaries	Maintaining professional distance
Following Up	Sending additional information after meetings
Using Visuals	Supporting ideas with charts or images
Being Open-Minded	Being willing to listen to new ideas and perspectives

Comprehension Questions:

1. What does active listening involve?

____

2. Why is it important to adapt your tone in the workplace?

____

3. How can body language improve communication?

____

4. When might following up be necessary?

____

5. Why is clarity essential in communication?

____

6. How does being open-minded support workplace communication?

____

Exercise 5- Read the HR email below before answering the questions.

From:	hr@xforce.com
To:	employees@xforce.com
Subject:	Performance Evaluations and Training Schedule

Dear Team,

We are excited to announce the upcoming schedule for performance evaluations and communication training sessions. These evaluations will help identify strengths and areas for improvement, ensuring we all strive for excellence. The communication training will cover topics such as active listening, feedback, and adapting tone for different situations.

Performance evaluations are scheduled for the first week of the month. Training sessions will be held bi-weekly on Wednesdays. Please review the attached schedule and plan accordingly. Let's work together to maintain a positive and effective communication culture in our workplace.

Best regards,
Human Resources
Xforce Inc.

Comprehension Questions:

1. What is the purpose of the email?

____

2. When are performance evaluations scheduled?

____

3. What topics will the communication training cover?

____

4. How often will training sessions take place?

____

5. Who is the letter from?

____

6. What is HR's goal for communication in the workplace?

____

Exercise 6- Fill in the blanks with the correct words: face-to-face, listening, evaluation, body, communication, and feedback.

1. The manager did an _________________________ to check each employee's performance.

2. A good _____________________ strategy includes adapting your tone based on the context.

3. Zoom meetings allow for _____________________ communication even from a distance.

4. Active _____________________ helps employees understand each other better.

5. Constructive _____________________ motivates employees to improve.

6. Face-to-face communication includes reading _____________________ language.

Exercise 7- Writing

Write two paragraphs to summarize what you know and learned about workplace communication in your own words.

ANSWER KEYS

Exercise 1- Vocabulary Matching:
1. Communication - b. The exchange of information between people
2. Strategy - h. A technique to achieve success
3. Evaluation - a. A process of assessing performance
4. Feedback - e. Guidance for improvement
5. Meeting - d. A gathering of people to discuss topics
6. Face-to-Face - g. In-person interaction
7. Zoom - f. An online video platform
8. Tone - c. The attitude or feeling shown in communication

Exercise 2- Text 1:
1. Face-to-face allows reading body language and getting immediate feedback.
2. Emails may lack tone and emotion, which can lead to misunderstandings.
3. Zoom is useful for remote work or global teams.
4. Email provides a written record of what was said, which can be useful for documentation.
5. The main idea is that different communication methods are essential in the workplace, each with its own advantages and challenges.
6. The author thinks Zoom is helpful because it lets people see each other, share ideas, and work together from different places.

Exercise 3- Text 2:
1. Active listening builds trust and understanding.
2. Feedback encourages personal and professional growth.
3. HR organizes training sessions to help employees learn communication strategies.
4. Written communication should avoid ambiguous language to prevent misunderstandings.
5. Changing tone ensures that communication is respectful and clear based on the situation.

6. The author believes feedback is very important because it helps employees grow and feel valued in their work.

Exercise 4- Workplace Communication Strategies:
1. Active listening means paying full attention to the speaker.
2. Adapting tone is important because it helps you communicate clearly and appropriately for the situation.
3. Body language improves spoken communication by showing feelings or support through gestures, facial expressions, and posture.
4. Follow up when additional information is needed.
5. Clarity helps others understand your message without confusion.
6. Being open-minded helps you listen to new ideas, which can lead to better teamwork and problem-solving.

Exercise 5- HR Email:
1. The purpose is to inform employees of evaluations and training.
2. They are scheduled for the first week of the month.
3. The training will cover active listening, feedback, and tone adaptation.
4. Training sessions will take place bi-weekly.
5. The letter is from Human Resources at Xforce Inc.
6. HR's goal is to maintain a positive and effective communication culture in the workplace.

Exercise 6- Fill-in-the-Blanks:
1. evaluation
2. communication
3. face-to-face
4. listening
5. feedback
6. body

REFLECTION ON LEARNING

Answer the following questions and discuss your responses with your teacher or classmates.

1. What reading strategies did you learn or practice in this unit?

2. What new concepts or words did you learn?

3. What reading challenges did you face?

4. What reading strategies do you need to improve?

5. What do you want your teacher to know?

Lesson 1: Voting and Elections in the US

Objectives:

1. Students will read and answer questions about the voting process and types of elections in the U.S.
2. Students will use new words to complete exercises about the importance of elections and voting.

Exercise 1- Draw a line connecting each word to its correct definition.

Word	Meaning
1. Ballot	a. A group of people with similar political beliefs
2. Candidate	b. A formal choice-making process
3. Election	c. Someone who runs for public office
4. Political Party	d. An election to choose a party's candidate for the general election
5. Campaign	e. A paper or electronic voting tool
6. Debate	f. A series of activities to win votes
7. Primary	g. A public discussion on issues
8. Voting Booth	h. A place to privately cast a vote

Exercise 2- Read the text below before answering the questions.

The Importance of Voting

Voting is one of the most important rights of citizens in a democracy. By voting, individuals have a voice in choosing their leaders and deciding the policies that impact their lives. In the U.S., citizens over the age of 18 have the right to vote in local, state, and national elections.

Elections happen at different levels, and each level has its own importance. Local elections, for example, affect community services, schools, and local policies. State and national elections determine the leaders who make bigger decisions. By voting, citizens participate in the democratic process and have a say in their government.

Political parties play a significant role in elections. Each party has a set of beliefs and goals. The two main political parties in the U.S. are the Democratic Party and the Republican Party. These parties help organize campaigns and debates to inform voters.

Comprehension Questions:

1. What is the main purpose of voting?

____

2. Why are local elections important?

____

3. What are the two main political parties in the U.S.?

____

4. What are the roles of political parties in elections?

____

5. What is the main idea of the text?

____

6. What is the author's view on the importance of voting?

____

Exercise 3- Read the text below before answering the questions.

Elections in the U.S.

In the U.S., there are several types of elections, including primary, general, and special elections. Primaries are held to select candidates for the general election. Each party holds its own primary, and voters choose which candidate they want to represent the party in the main election.

The general election is held every four years for the presidency and every two years for Congress. In this election, voters decide who will hold public office at the national and state levels. Special elections are held to fill vacant positions outside of the regular schedule.

Each type of election has its own schedule and purpose. For instance, primaries are scheduled months before the general election. Understanding the types of elections helps citizens know when and why to participate in the democratic process.

Comprehension Questions:

1. What is the purpose of primary elections?

____

2. How often is the general election held for the presidency?

____

3. What are special elections used for?

____

4. Why are primaries scheduled before the general election?

____

5. What is the main idea of the text?

____

6. Why does the author describe the different types of elections?

____

Exercise 4- Read the text below before answering the questions.

Political Campaigns and Debates

Political campaigns are an organized effort by candidates to win votes. A campaign includes various activities, such as speeches, advertisements, and rallies. The goal is to reach as many voters as possible and convince them to support the candidate.

Debates are a key part of campaigns, where candidates discuss important issues. Debates give voters a chance to hear the candidates' views and compare their positions. By listening to debates, voters can make informed decisions about whom to support.

Campaigns and debates play a crucial role in elections. They provide information, create awareness, and help voters understand each candidate's policies. Informed voting is essential to a healthy democracy, and campaigns are a way to educate the public.

Comprehension Questions:

1. What is the purpose of a political campaign?

____

2. How do debates help voters?

____

3. Why are campaigns important for democracy?

____

4. What is the main goal of a campaign?

____

5. What is the main idea of the text?

____

6. What is the author's opinion on informed voting?

____

Exercise 5- Read the types of elections below before answering the questions.

Types of Elections

Election Type	Schedule	Importance
Primary	Months before the general election	Selects party candidates
General	Every four years (presidency)	Elects leaders for public office
Midterm	Every two years	Elects members of Congress
Special	As needed	Fills vacancies outside of the regular schedule
Local	Varies by state and city	Affects community policies and services

Comprehension Questions:

1. What is the purpose of the primary election?

____

2. How often is the general election for the presidency held?

____

3. Why might a special election be necessary?

____

4. What is the focus of local elections?

____

5. Why is understanding the election schedule important?

____

6. How do midterm elections differ from general elections?

____

Exercise 6- Read the campaign ad below before answering the questions.

Campaign Ad

Candidates	Experience	Policies	Endorsements
Candidate A	10 years in public service	Focus on education reform	Teachers' Union
Candidate B	Business leader	Economic growth and job creation	Small Business Network

Comprehension Questions:

1. What is Candidate A's main focus?

____

2. What background does Candidate B have?

____

3. Which candidate is endorsed by the Teachers' Union?

____

4. How do the candidates' policies differ?

____

5. What is the purpose of endorsements in campaigns?

____

6. What can voters learn from this comparison?

____

Exercise 7- Fill in the blanks with the correct words: political party, campaign, debate, ballot, general and voting booth.

1. A _____________________________ is a public discussion where candidates share their views.

2. The _____________________________ election decides who will take public office.

3. A _____________________________ helps inform voters about a candidate's policies.

4. In the U.S., citizens cast their vote in a _____________________________.

5. A _____________________________ is a private space to vote without interference.

6. Each _____________________________ has its own set of beliefs and values.

Exercise 8- Writing

Write two paragraphs to summarize what you know and learned about voting and elections in your own words.

ANSWER KEYS

Exercise 1- Vocabulary Matching:
1. Ballot - e. A paper or electronic voting tool
2. Candidate - c. Someone who runs for public office
3. Election - b. A formal choice-making process
4. Political Party - a. A group of people with similar political beliefs
5. Campaign - f. A series of activities to win votes
6. Debate - g. A public discussion on issues
7. Primary - d. An election to choose a party's candidate for the general election
8. Voting Booth - h. A place to privately cast a vote

Exercise 2- Text 1:
1. Voting allows citizens to choose leaders and decide on policies that affect their lives.
2. Local elections impact community services, schools and local policies.
3. The two main parties are the Democratic Party and the Republican Party.
4. Parties organize campaigns and debates to inform voters about the candidates.
5. Voting is an important right that lets people choose leaders and help make decisions for the country.
6. The author believes voting is an essential right as citizens can choose their leaders and have a say in policies that affect them.

Exercise 3- Text 2:
1. Primary elections select party candidates.
2. The general election for the presidency is held every four years.
3. Special elections are used to fill vacant government positions.
4. Primaries are held before to select the candidate for the general election.
5. Understanding elections helps citizens know when and why to participate in elections.
6. The author mentions different types of elections to show that each has a specific purpose and schedule.

Exercise 4- Text 3:
1. A campaign aims to win votes.
2. Debates let voters compare candidates' positions.
3. Campaigns educate the public.
4. The main goal is to convince voters to support the candidate.
5. Campaigns and debates inform voters and support democracy.
6. Informed voting is essential for a healthy democracy.

Exercise 5- Types of Elections:
1. Primary elections select party candidates.
2. The general election for presidency is every four years.
3. Special elections are held to fill vacancies outside of the regular election schedule.
4. Local elections impact community decisions.
5. Understanding the schedule helps citizens know when to vote and what positions are being filled.
6. Midterms are held every two years to elect Congress members. Meanwhile, general elections are held every four years to elect leaders for public office.

Exercise 6- Campaign Ads:
1. Candidate A focuses on education reform.
2. Candidate B is a business leader.
3. Candidate A is endorsed by the Teachers' Union.
4. Candidate A focuses on education, and B on the economy.
5. Endorsements show support from groups and build credibility.
6. Voters learn candidates' backgrounds, policies, and endorsements to help make an informed decision.

Exercise 7- Fill-in-the-Blanks:
1. debate
2. general
3. campaign
4. ballot
5. voting booth
6. political party

Lesson 2: Economy and Finances

Objectives:

1. Students will read and answer questions about economics, including online banking, stock market, budgeting, and investment.
2. Students will use new words to complete exercises about types of bank and investment accounts and types of loans used in daily life.

Exercise 1- Draw a line connecting each word to its correct definition.

Words	Meaning
1. Investment	a. Money borrowed to be repaid with interest
2. Budgeting	b. A record of financial transactions
3. Stock Market	c. Money set aside for future needs
4. Loan	d. A long-term loan for property purchase
5. Interest	e. A place where shares are bought and sold
6. Account	f. Setting aside money for future growth
7. Mortgage	g. Planning and organizing income and expenses
8. Savings	h. The cost paid for borrowing money

Exercise 2- Read the text below before answering the questions.

Online Banking

Online banking allows individuals to manage their finances from their computers or smartphones. With online banking, users can check their balances, transfer money, and pay bills, making it easier to manage money without visiting a bank.

Security is a crucial aspect of online banking. Banks use encryption and extra security checks to protect users' data. However, users must be careful with their passwords and avoid sharing their information with others.

Many banks offer additional online services, such as tools for budgeting and investment planning. These services allow people to keep track of their spending and save for the future, giving them greater control over their financial health.

Comprehension Questions:

1. What is the main benefit of online banking?

____

2. How does online banking ensure security?

____

3. Why should users keep their passwords secret?

____

4. What additional tools do banks offer for online users?

____

5. What is the main idea of this text?

____

6. What is the author's perspective on online banking?

____

Exercise 3- Read the text below before answering the questions.

The Stock Market

The stock market is a place where individuals and institutions buy and sell shares of companies. Investing in stocks allows people to own a small part of a company, with the potential to earn profits as the company grows.

However, investing in the stock market comes with risks. Prices of stocks can rise and fall due to economic changes, company performance, and global events. It's important for investors to research before investing to avoid losses.

For many, the stock market is a way to grow wealth over time. Those who understand how it works can make informed decisions and potentially gain financial security by investing wisely.

Comprehension Questions:

1. What does investing in the stock market allow people to do?

____

2. Why is the stock market risky?

____

3. What factors affect stock prices?

____

4. How can investors reduce the risk of loss?

____

5. What is the main idea of this text?

____

6. What does the author believe about investing long-term in the stock market?

____

The Importance of Budgeting

Budgeting is the process of organizing income and expenses to make the best use of money. By setting a budget, people can ensure that they have enough for their needs and save for their future goals.

Creating a budget involves listing all sources of income and then deciding how much to put aside for expenses, savings, and other financial goals. This can help individuals avoid overspending and build a habit of saving.

Budgeting not only helps with day-to-day financial management but also prepares individuals for unexpected expenses. Those who budget are often less stressed about money and have a better chance of achieving long-term financial stability.

Comprehension Questions:

1. What is the purpose of budgeting?

____

2. How does budgeting help with saving?

____

3. What are the basic steps in creating a budget?

____

4. How can budgeting reduce financial stress?

____

5. What is the main idea of this text?

____

6. Why does the author explain the process of budgeting?

____

Exercise 5- Read the bank and investment accounts below before answering the questions.

Bank and Investment Accounts

Account Type	Purpose	Minimum Balance	Interest Rate
Checking Account	Daily transactions	$25	0.01%
Savings Account	Savings for future	$100	0.10%
Money Market	Higher interest savings	$500	0.25%
CD (Certificate)	Fixed-term savings	$1000	1.00%
IRA	Retirement savings	Varies	1.5%

Comprehension Questions:

1. Which account is typically used for daily transactions?

____

2. What is the minimum balance required for a Money Market account?

____

3. Which account type has the highest interest rate?

____

4. What is the primary purpose of a CD?

____

5. What kind of account is specifically for retirement savings?

____

6. Why might someone choose a Savings Account over a Checking Account?

____

Exercise 6- Read the bank and investment accounts below before answering the questions.

Loans for Andrea Stevenson

Loan Type	Balance Due	Due Date	Interest Rate
Auto Loan	$5,000	12/15/2024	4.0%
Mortgage	$120,000	01/01/2025	3.5%
Personal Loan	$3,000	11/20/2024	6.5%
Credit Card	$1,200	11/10/2024	18.0%
Student Loan	$10,000	12/01/2024	5.0%

Comprehension Questions:

1. Which loan has the highest interest rate?

____

2. What is the due date for the mortgage payment?

____

3. How much balance does Andrea owe on her auto loan?

____

4. Which loan has the lowest interest rate?

____

5. What is the main purpose of a student loan?

____

6. Why might someone choose a personal loan over a credit card loan?

____

Exercise 7- Fill in the blanks with the correct words: budget, loan, stock market, investment, interest, and checking account.

1. To grow my money, I am considering an _______________________________.

2. A _______________________________ helps me organize my expenses and income.

3. The _______________________________ is a place where shares are bought and sold.

4. A _______________________________ is money borrowed that must be repaid with interest.

5. _______________________________ is the cost of borrowing money.

6. I keep my daily funds in a _______________________________.

Exercise 8- Writing

Write two paragraphs to summarize what you know and learned about economy and finances in your own words.

ANSWER KEYS

Exercise 1- Vocabulary Matching:
1. Investment - f. Setting aside money for future growth
2. Budgeting - g. Planning and organizing income and expenses
3. Stock Market - e. A place where shares are bought and sold
4. Loan - a. Money borrowed to be repaid with interest
5. Interest - h. The cost paid for borrowing money
6. Account - b. A record of financial transactions
7. Mortgage - d. A long-term loan for property purchase
8. Savings - c. Money set aside for future needs

Exercise 2- Text 1:
1. It allows individuals to manage their finances without visiting a bank.
2. Online banking uses encryption and extra security checks.
3. Users should keep their passwords secret to protect their accounts from unauthorized access.
4. Banks offer tools for budgeting and investment planning.
5. Online banking is convenient and helps users manage their money securely.
6. The author views online banking as a convenient and secure way to manage finances.

Exercise 3- Text 2:
1. It allows people to own a part of a company and potentially earn profits.
2. It is risky because stock prices can rise and fall due to various factors.
3. Economic changes, company performance, and global events affect stock prices.
4. They can reduce the risk by researching before investing.
5. The stock market can help people grow their money over time, but it has risks.
6. The author believes that investing long-term can help people grow their wealth over time if approached wisely.

Exercise 4- Text 3:
1. The purpose is to organize income and expenses effectively.
2. Budgeting allows people to put aside money for future goals and avoid overspending.
3. The basic steps in creating a budget are listing all sources of income and deciding how much to spend.
4. It helps prepare for unexpected expenses and provides financial stability.
5. Budgeting is important for managing money, reducing stress, and achieving long-term financial stability.
6. The author explains the process to help readers understand how to organize their income and expenses.

Exercise 5- Bank and Investment Accounts
1. The checking account is mostly used for daily transactions.
2. The minimum balance is $500.
3. The IRA has the highest interest rate.
4. The CD is for fixed-term savings.
5. The IRA is specifically for retirement savings.
6. They might do this so they could save money with interest.

Exercise 6- Loans for Andrea Stevenson
1. The credit card has the highest interest rate.
2. The mortgage payment is due on 01/01/2025.
3. She owes $5,000.
4. The mortgage has the lowest interest rate.
5. The student loan funds education costs.
6. They might do so for the lower interest rate.

Exercise 7- Fill in the Blanks:
1. investment
2. budget
3. stock market
4. loan
5. interest
6. checking account

REFLECTION ON LEARNING

Answer the following questions and discuss your responses with your teacher or classmates.

1. What reading strategies did you learn or practice in this unit?

2. What new concepts or words did you learn?

3. What reading challenges did you face?

4. What reading strategies do you need to improve?

5. What do you want your teacher to know?

You have 70 minutes to answer 40 questions.

Section 1: Read the text before choosing the correct answers to questions 1 to 4.

The Role of Community Agencies in Our Lives

Community agencies provide a variety of services that help individuals and families in many ways. In the United States, agencies such as food banks, health clinics, and housing services offer essential support to people in need. These agencies often work with the local government to provide resources for those who are unemployed, homeless, or struggling to make ends meet.

Another important agency is the job assistance center. These types of centers provide training programs, resume workshops, and job listings to help people find employment. By offering these services, they empower individuals to improve their financial situation and contribute to the community.

Additionally, community health clinics are available to offer affordable healthcare to people without insurance. They provide basic medical care, vaccinations, and sometimes mental health support. This ensures that even low-income families have access to necessary healthcare, improving the overall health of the community.

Comprehension Questions:

1. What is the main idea of the text?

   A) Community agencies help only with job training.

   B) Community agencies are essential for providing a range of support services.

   C) Healthcare clinics are the only important community agencies.

   D) Community agencies work alone without government support.

2. What is the author's purpose in this text?

   A) To inform readers about the different types of community agencies and their roles

   B) To persuade readers to donate to community agencies

   C) To criticize the lack of support from community agencies

   D) To explain the process of setting up a community agency

3. What can be inferred about the job assistance center?

A) It only helps with job listings.

B) It is essential for helping people improve their financial stability.

C) It primarily provides medical care.

D) It works without local government support.

4. Why might community health clinics be particularly important for low-income families?

A) They offer financial support.

B) They provide basic healthcare at an affordable cost.

C) They offer job training programs.

D) They work with food banks.

Section 2: Read the text before choosing the correct answers to questions 5 to 7.

Protecting Yourself as a Consumer

In today's world, it's essential for consumers to understand their rights and how to protect themselves. One way to do this is by understanding the terms and conditions of any purchase or contract. Reading the fine print helps consumers avoid hidden fees or clauses that could cost them later.

Another important practice is checking reviews and ratings before buying a product or service. Websites like Consumer Reports and the Better Business Bureau provide valuable information about a company's reputation. This helps consumers make informed decisions and avoid potential scams.

Finally, consumers should always keep records of their purchases, especially for big-ticket items. Receipts and warranties can be crucial if there is a problem with the product. Knowing your rights and keeping documentation can help resolve issues quickly and efficiently.

Comprehension Questions:

5. What is the main idea of the article?

A) Consumer protection laws are too strict.

B) Consumers should understand their rights and how to protect themselves.

C) Businesses should keep records for their customers.

D) Reviews are unnecessary when making purchases.

6. According to the article, why is reading the fine print important?

    A) It helps avoid unexpected costs or conditions.

    B) It guarantees a better product.

    C) It allows consumers to return items easily.

    D) It provides an extended warranty.

7. What is suggested about websites like Consumer Reports?

    A) They only publish negative reviews.

    B) They work for the government.

    C) They help consumers make informed decisions.

    D) They are funded by the companies they review.

Section 3: Read the text before choosing the correct answers to questions 8 to 10.

Leisure Time Options

Leisure time activities are essential for maintaining a balanced lifestyle. In many communities, residents can enjoy facilities like gyms, libraries, and parks. For example, the local YMCA offers various programs, including fitness classes, swimming lessons, and after-school programs for children.

Sports facilities are also available in many areas. These include soccer fields, basketball courts, and even skate parks. Participating in sports is not only a great way to stay fit but also helps people build connections within their community.

For those who prefer quieter activities, libraries provide a peaceful environment to read, study, or attend workshops. Many libraries also offer free internet access and computer classes, making them valuable resources for learning and personal growth.

Comprehension Questions:

8. What is the main idea of the text?

    A) Libraries are the most important leisure facility.

    B) Community resources offer various activities for physical and personal growth.

    C) Only children benefit from leisure resources.

    D) Sports facilities are more beneficial than libraries.

9. What can be inferred about the YMCA?

    A) It only offers swimming lessons.

    B) It is a resource for community programs that include physical activities.

    C) It focuses mainly on competitive sports.

    D) It is a private sports club.

10. Why might libraries be particularly valuable for some community members?

    A) They offer free access to learning resources.

    B) They are a good place for sports.

    C) They provide food and drinks.

    D) They are open 24 hours a day.

Section 4: Read the text before choosing the correct answers to questions 11 to 13.

The U.S. Education System

The U.S. education system includes a variety of schools and programs designed to meet the needs of students at different stages. From early childhood programs like Head Start to elementary, middle, and high schools, the focus is on providing a foundational education.

Community colleges offer an affordable path for students who wish to pursue higher education or technical skills. Many students start at community colleges and then transfer to four-year universities to complete their degrees.

Additionally, there are adult education programs available for those who want to continue their learning later in life. These programs provide training in language skills, job skills, and other areas to help adults meet their goals.

Comprehension Questions:

11. What is the main purpose of the U.S. education system, according to the text?

    A) To make education expensive

    B) To limit higher education to young people

    C) To prepare students only for technical careers

    D) To provide a range of programs for students of all ages

12. What role do community colleges play in the education system?

    A) They provide free education for all.

    B) They offer an affordable option for higher education.

    C) They focus only on technical training.

    D) They are available only for adults.

13. What can be inferred about adult education programs?

    A) They are primarily for children.

    B) They are the same as high school programs.

    C) They help adults develop new skills.

    D) They are not widely available.

Section 5: Read the text before choosing the correct answers to questions 14 to 16.

Choosing the Right Medication for Your Needs

Selecting the right medication can be overwhelming with so many options available. It's essential to consult a pharmacist or doctor before making any decisions, especially if you have existing health conditions. They can advise on dosage and possible side effects.

Over-the-counter medications are available for minor health issues. However, prescription drugs require approval from a healthcare provider. Understanding the difference is essential so you can use medicines safely.

Furthermore, it's important to read labels and follow instructions carefully to prevent adverse effects. Proper medication use not only treats symptoms but also contributes to overall health and well-being.

Comprehension Questions:

14. What is the main idea of this text?

    A) Reading labels is the most important step in choosing medication.

    B) Choosing the right medication requires proper guidance and understanding.

    C) Over-the-counter medications are always safe for everyone.

    D) Prescription drugs are not necessary for treating health issues.

15. Why should one consult a pharmacist or doctor?

   A) They help patients avoid all medications.

   B) They provide free medications.

   C) They can recommend the correct dosage and state the side effects.

   D) They provide financial support for medications.

16. What is the author's view on reading medication labels?

   A) It is unnecessary.

   B) It is only for pharmacists to read.

   C) It only applies to prescription drugs.

   D) It prevents adverse effects.

Section 6: Read the text before choosing the correct answers to questions 17 to 19.

Healthcare Providers and Services

In the United States, there are various healthcare providers to meet the needs of the community. Family doctors, also known as primary care physicians (PCPs), offer general medical care and refer patients to specialists if needed. These specialists, such as cardiologists and dermatologists, focus on specific areas of health.

Hospitals provide emergency care, surgeries, and long-term treatment options. Patients may also visit clinics for minor medical issues, vaccinations, or check-ups, which are often more affordable than hospitals. Pharmacies are an essential part of the healthcare system, offering medications and advice on their use.

Dentists and optometrists are also available for dental and eye health. Together, these healthcare providers ensure comprehensive care for all aspects of a person's well-being.

Comprehension Questions:

17. What is the main idea of this text?

   A) Various healthcare providers meet different health needs in the U.S.

   B) Hospitals are the only healthcare providers people should visit.

   C) Pharmacies provide emergency care.

   D) Only specialists can provide proper healthcare.

18. According to the text, what is the role of a primary care physician?

   A) To perform surgeries

   B) To provide specialized healthcare

   C) To offer general care and refer to specialists if needed

   D) To work only in hospitals

19. Why might clinics be a good option for patients?

   A) They are more affordable for minor issues.

   B) They only provide emergency care.

   C) They specialize in surgeries.

   D) They are available only for vaccinations.

Section 7: Read the text before choosing the correct answers to questions 20 to 23.

Finding Employment

Finding a job can be challenging, but there are effective strategies that can help. Networking is one of the best ways to discover job opportunities. By connecting with professionals in your field, you can learn about job openings that may not be advertised.

Online job boards like LinkedIn and Indeed have also made it easier to find employment. They allow job seekers to create profiles, upload resumes, and apply for jobs with just a few clicks. Job fairs, both virtual and in-person, are another resource for job seekers to meet employers and learn about potential careers.

It's important to be prepared for interviews by practicing answers to common questions and researching the company. These strategies can help job seekers stand out in a competitive job market and increase their chances of getting hired.

Comprehension Questions:

20. What is the main idea of this text?

   A) Finding a job is impossible in today's market.

   B) Networking and online platforms are key strategies for job searching.

   C) Job fairs are outdated.

   D) Only online job boards help in finding a job.

21. What can be inferred about job fairs?

    A) They are rarely attended by employers.

    B) They are useful for meeting potential employers.

    C) They only offer jobs in specific industries.

    D) They are held exclusively online.

22. Why is it important to research a company before an interview?

    A) It guarantees a job offer.

    B) It helps job seekers prepare better.

    C) It reduces the need for practicing answers.

    D) It increases the salary offered.

23. What is the author's purpose in this text?

    A) To inform readers about effective job search strategies

    B) To persuade readers to attend only online job boards

    C) To criticize traditional job-searching methods

    D) To describe job offers available in specific industries

Section 8: Read the text before choosing the correct answers to questions 24 to 27.

Employee Benefits and Rights

In the workplace, employees are entitled to certain rights and benefits. Wages should meet minimum wage standards and be paid on time. Employees also have the right to a safe work environment, free from harassment and discrimination.

Benefits such as health insurance, retirement plans, and paid time off are often provided by employers to support the well-being of their employees. Understanding these benefits can help employees make informed decisions about job offers and contracts.

Unions are organizations that advocate for workers' rights and fair treatment. Union members may benefit from collective bargaining, which can lead to better wages, improved working conditions, and other benefits.

Comprehension Questions:

24. What is the main idea of this text?

    A) Employers do not offer enough benefits.

    B) Employees have rights and can benefit from unions.

    C) All jobs provide equal benefits.

    D) Minimum wage is the only right employees have.

25. Why are unions beneficial for employees?

    A) They reduce wages.

    B) They replace employer-provided benefits.

    C) They guarantee promotions.

    D) They help negotiate better conditions and benefits.

26. What is the author's purpose in this text?

    A) To inform employees about their rights and available benefits

    B) To encourage employees to work without benefits

    C) To persuade employers to remove benefits

    D) To criticize employees who do not join unions

27. What can be inferred about benefits like health insurance and retirement plans?

    A) They are mandatory for all employers.

    B) They support employee well-being and future planning.

    C) They are not helpful to employees.

    D) They are only available in large companies.

Section 9: Read the text before choosing the correct answers to questions 28 to 30.

Job Performance and Training

In today's fast-paced work environment, continuous training is essential for employees to stay updated with new skills. Many companies offer mandatory training sessions on topics like safety, IT skills, and equal employment opportunities.

Training helps employees improve their job performance and contributes to personal development. It also boosts confidence by equipping employees with the skills needed to perform their roles effectively.

Additionally, some companies provide optional training programs to help employees advance in their careers. By taking advantage of these opportunities, employees can achieve both personal and professional growth.

Comprehension Questions:

28. What is the main purpose of job training, according to the text?

    A) To replace traditional job roles

    B) To improve job performance and personal growth

    C) To increase employee salaries

    D) To reduce the workforce

29. What can be inferred about optional training programs?

    A) They are only available in specific industries.

    B) They help employees grow in their careers.

    C) They are mandatory for all employees.

    D) They are not useful for employees.

30. What is the author's purpose in this text?

    A) To inform readers about the benefits of job training

    B) To discourage employees from attending training

    C) To criticize companies that do not offer training

    D) To promote specific training programs

Section 10: Read the text before choosing the correct answers to questions 31 to 32.

Communication in the Workplace

Good communication is crucial for a productive work environment. Strategies such as active listening, clear instructions, and feedback help ensure that team members understand each other.

Face-to-face meetings are useful for discussing complex issues, while emails are efficient for quick updates. Virtual platforms like Zoom allow teams to connect, especially if they work remotely.

By practicing these strategies, employees can improve teamwork, reduce misunderstandings, and foster a positive workplace culture.

Comprehension Questions:

31. What is the main idea of this text?

    A) Communication is only important in virtual teams.

    B) Effective communication strategies are essential for workplace success.

    C) Face-to-face meetings are ineffective.

    D) Emails should be avoided in the workplace.

32. Why might Zoom be useful in a workplace setting?

    A) It allows face-to-face communication for remote teams.

    B) It replaces all other forms of communication.

    C) It is only for in-office teams.

    D) It limits misunderstandings completely.

Section 11: Read the text before choosing the correct answers to questions 33 to 36.

The Voting Process in the U.S.

In the United States, voting is a critical part of the democratic process. Citizens have the right to vote in local, state, and national elections. Voting allows individuals to choose leaders who represent their values and to voice their opinions on important issues.

The political system includes different types of elections. Presidential elections occur every four years. Meanwhile, congressional and local elections may take place every two years. Many states also have primary elections, where political parties select their candidates for the general election.

Political parties play a significant role in organizing and encouraging voters. In the U.S., the two major parties are the Democratic Party and the Republican Party. Each party has its own platform, which outlines its views on issues like healthcare, education, and the economy. By participating in the political process, citizens can influence policies that affect their lives.

Comprehension Questions:

33. What is the main idea of this text?

    A) Only the President can make decisions for the U.S.

    B) Only local elections affect citizens.

    C) Voting only happens every four years.

    D) Voting allows citizens to participate in the democratic process.

34. What can be inferred about primary elections?

    A) They are the only type of election in the U.S.

    B) They allow political parties to select candidates.

    C) They are unimportant to the political process.

    D) They are the same as general elections.

35. According to the text, what is a major function of political parties?

    A) To organize and encourage voters

    B) To decide who wins the election

    C) To govern all states

    D) To limit voting rights

36. What is the author's purpose in this text?

    A) To inform readers about the importance of voting and political parties

    B) To persuade readers to vote in local elections only

    C) To criticize the Democratic and Republican parties

    D) To discourage voting in presidential elections

Section 12: Read the text before choosing the correct answers to questions 37 to 40.

Managing Personal Finances

Managing personal finances is an important skill in today's economy. Online banking has become popular, allowing people to check their balances, transfer funds, and even deposit checks from their mobile devices. This convenience helps people manage their money without visiting a bank in person.

The stock market offers another way to manage and grow finances. People can invest in stocks and bonds, which may increase in value over time. However, the stock market carries risks, so it's important to invest carefully and understand the potential for both gains and losses.

Budgeting is a crucial skill for managing finances. By setting a budget, people can track their income and expenses, ensuring that they don't overspend. Budgeting helps individuals save for the future and avoid debt. Investments like stocks, real estate, and retirement accounts can also contribute to financial stability if managed wisely.

Comprehension Questions:

37. What is the main purpose of online banking according to the text?

    A) To help people manage their money without visiting a bank

    B) To encourage people to spend more money

    C) To prevent people from using checks

    D) To replace budgeting as a financial tool

38. What can be inferred about the stock market?

    A) It is a guaranteed way to make money.

    B) It offers potential for financial growth but carries risks.

    C) It is only for wealthy individuals.

    D) It is safer than budgeting.

39. According to the text, why is budgeting important?

    A) It helps people track their income and expenses.

    B) It eliminates the need for investments.

    C) It ensures everyone becomes wealthy.

    D) It allows people to ignore their income.

40. What is the author's purpose in this text?

    A) To inform readers about personal finance tools and concepts

    B) To discourage people from using online banking

    C) To promote investments over budgeting

    D) To criticize the stock market

ANSWER KEY:

Section 1: The Role of Community Agencies in Our Lives

 1- B
 2- A
 3- B
 4- B

Section 2: Protecting Yourself as a Consumer

 5- B
 6- A
 7- C

Section 3: Leisure Time Options

 8- B
 9- B
 10- A

Section 4: The U.S. Education System

 11- D
 12- B
 13- C

Section 5: Choosing the Right Medication for Your Needs

 14- B
 15- C
 16- D

Section 6: Healthcare Providers and Services

 17- A
 18- C
 19- A

Section 7: Finding Employment

 20- B
 21- B
 22- B
 23- A

Section 8: Employee Benefits and Rights

 24- B
 25- D
 26- A
 27- B

Section 9: Job Performance and Training

 28- C
 29- B
 30- A

Section 10: Communication in the Workplace

 31- B
 32- A

Section 11: The Voting Process in the U.S.

 33- D
 34- B
 35- A
 36- A

Section 12: Managing Personal Finances

 37- A
 38- B
 39- A
 40- A

CASAS
TEST PREP
STUDENT
BOOK
FOR
MATH GOALS FORM
913 M LEVEL A/B
By Coaching for Better Learning, LLC

CASAS
TEST PREP
STUDENT
BOOK
FOR
MATH GOALS FORM
914 M LEVEL A/B
By Coaching for Better Learning, LLC

CASAS
TEST PREP
STUDENT
BOOK
FOR
MATH GOALS FORM
917 M LEVEL C/D
By Coaching for Better Learning, LLC

CASAS
TEST PREP
STUDENT
BOOK
FOR
MATH GOALS FORM
918 M LEVEL C/D
By Coaching for Better Learning, LLC

CASAS
TEST PREP
STUDENT
BOOK
FOR
READING GOALS
FORM 901R/902R
LEVEL A
By Coaching for Better Learning, LLC

CASAS
TEST PREP
STUDENT
BOOK
FOR
READING GOALS
FORM 903R/904R
LEVEL B
By Coaching for Better Learning, LLC

CASAS
TEST PREP
STUDENT
BOOK
FOR
READING GOALS
FORM 905R/906R
LEVEL C
By Coaching for Better Learning, LLC

CASAS
TEST PREP
STUDENT
BOOK
FOR
READING GOALS
FORM 907R/908R
LEVEL D
By Coaching for Better Learning, LLC

TEST PREP MATH BOOK
FOR
CASAS Math GOALS 2
Level A—Forms 921M and 922M
CBL COACHING

TEST PREP MATH BOOK
FOR
CASAS Math GOALS 2
Level E—Forms 929M and 930M
CBL COACHING

TEST PREP MATH BOOK
FOR
CASAS Math GOALS 2
Level C—Forms 925M and 926M
CBL COACHING

Test Prep Reading Book
for
CASAS Reading STEPS
Level B—Forms 623R & 624R
CBL

Test Prep Reading Book
for
CASAS Reading STEPS
Level C—Forms 625R & 626R
CBL

Test Prep Reading Book
for
CASAS Reading STEPS
Level A—Forms 621R & 622R
CBL

LEARNING
& STUDY GUIDE
FOR ADULT STUDENTS
CBL COACHING
By Coaching for Better Learning

LEARNING
& STUDY GUIDE
FOR ADULT STUDENTS
Bundle: Student Guide & Teacher's Manual
CBL COACHING
By Coaching for Better Learning, LLC

TABE
11 & 12
STUDENT MATH MANUAL
AND PRACTICE TESTS
FOR LEVEL D
Preparing Adult Learners
to Ace TABE 11 & 12 Math Test Level D
By Coaching for Better Learning, LLC

TABE
11 & 12
STUDENT MATH MANUAL
AND PRACTICE TESTS
FOR LEVEL E
Preparing Adult Learners
to Ace TABE 11 & 12 Math Test Level E
By Coaching for Better Learning, LLC

TABE
11 & 12
STUDENT MATH MANUAL
AND PRACTICE TESTS
FOR LEVEL M
Preparing Adult Learners
to Ace TABE 11 & 12 Math Test Level M
By Coaching for Better Learning, LLC

GED
Math Study
Guide
FOCUSING ON
MATHEMATICAL REASONING
AND THINKING
By Coaching for Better Learning, LLC

ADULT ED
MATH
NUMBER SYSTEM, NUMBER SENSE, AND OPERATIONS PREPARING
FOR
CASAS, TABE 11 & 12, HISET, AND GED TESTING
BY COACHING FOR BETTER LEARNING

ADULT ED
MATH
GEOMETRY PREPARING
FOR
CASAS, TABE 11 & 12, HISET, AND GED TESTING
BY COACHING FOR BETTER LEARNING

CBL COACHING
Math
Practice Worksheets and Workbook for Adult Students

SKILLS FOR SUCCESS IN CAREER AND TECHNICAL EDUCATION (CTE)
STUDENT GUIDE
A SYSTEMATIC WAY TO MASTER ORGANIZATIONAL AND SOFT SKILLS
CBL COACHING

HOW TO ACHIEVE BETTER STUDENT RETENTION IN ADULT EDUCATION
TEDDY EDOUARD

TABE 11 & 12
CONSUMABLE STUDENT READING MANUAL
FOR LEVEL E
By Coaching for Better Learning, LLC

TABE 11 & 12
CONSUMABLE STUDENT READING MANUAL
FOR LEVEL M
By Coaching for Better Learning, LLC

TABE 11 & 12
CONSUMABLE STUDENT READING MANUAL
FOR LEVEL D
By Coaching for Better Learning, LLC

TABE 11 & 12
STUDENT LANGUAGE MANUAL
FOR LEVEL E
By Coaching for Better Learning, LLC

TABE 11 & 12
STUDENT LANGUAGE MANUAL
FOR LEVEL M
By Coaching for Better Learning, LLC

TABE 11 & 12
Consumable Student Math Workbook
FOR LEVEL E
By Coaching for Better Learning, LLC

TABE 11 & 12
Consumable Student Math Workbook
FOR LEVEL M
By Coaching for Better Learning, LLC

TABE 11 & 12
Consumable Student Math Workbook
FOR LEVEL D
By Coaching for Better Learning, LLC

PRACTICE TESTS FOR CASAS MATH GOAL 2
CBL COACHING

CBL COACHING
Workbook
Number and Letter Tracing for Adult Students

READING NOTEBOOK & JOURNAL
For Adult Students
By Coaching For Better Learning   CBL COACHING

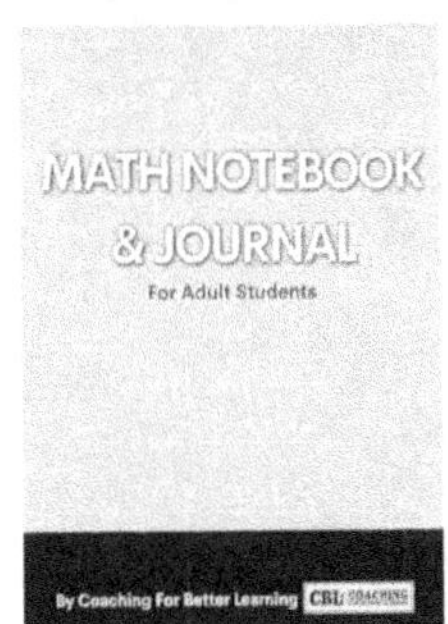

MATH NOTEBOOK & JOURNAL
For Adult Students
By Coaching For Better Learning   CBL COACHING

BOOK 1
PHONICS AND LIFE SKILLS READING
FOR
Adult Literacy, ABE, and ESL Students
Turning Learners into Proficient Readers
CBL COACHING

BOOK 2
PHONICS AND LIFE SKILLS READING
FOR
Adult Literacy, ABE, and ESL Students
Turning Learners into Proficient Readers
CBL COACHING

BOOK 3
PHONICS AND LIFE SKILLS READING
FOR
Adult Literacy, ABE, and ESL Students
Turning Learners into Proficient Readers
CBL COACHING

ABOUT CBL

At CBL, we promote systematic solutions, learner-centered textbooks, and forward-thinking strategies in adult education, workforce development, and vocational training. Our diverse solutions and products are intricately designed to enrich students' learning experiences while making the job of busy, hard-working adult instructors easier.

CBL takes pride in publishing student-centered textbooks designed to prepare learners for CASAS, TABE 11&12, HiSET, and GED assessments and to assist instructors in covering course curricula and standards with confidence.

Our publications also include teaching guides, test prep tools, and study guides that foster reflective learning, ensuring sustained engagement in active learning. Find our meticulously crafted textbooks on our book page (cbledu.com) or major platforms like Amazon, Barnes & Noble, and Ingram Spark.

CBL also guides adult education and workforce programs in establishing robust professional development programs—training, peer-mentoring, coaching, community of practices (CoPs), and instructional systems— fostering a culture of continuous improvement and contributing to higher learner retention and success rates. We also offer workshops and PD sessions for adult educators and classroom instructors.

If you have questions about instructional systems, textbooks, or student learning and retention, contact us today at teamcbl@cbledu.com or 410-960-4082.